The Fallen Autumn

FIRST EDITION – 5
Copyright © 2025 by Nathan Brown
All Rights Reserved
ISBN-13: 979-8-9881271-5-4

Library of Congress Control Number:
2025931765

No part of this book may be performed, recorded, thieved, or otherwise transmitted without the written consent of the author and the permission of the publisher. However, portions may be cited for book reviews—favorable or otherwise—without obtaining consent.

Mezcalita Press, LLC, Norman, Oklahoma

Cover Design: Chris Everett

MEZCALITA
PRESS

Norman, Oklahoma

The Fallen Autumn

The Birth of a Vagabond
Book 2

Nathan Brown

MEZCALITA
PRESS

Table of Contents

An Introduction

The Fallen Autumn—Book 2 in the series of *The Birth of a Vagabond*—follows up on the shatter and bottoming-out of the trials and errors portrayed in *The Broken Summer* with a journey that begins with bare feet and moonbeams down in the American Heartland, but soon heads over and up to the Pacific coastline, rivers, and small mountain towns of Oregon—and then back again to the southern reaches of the Great Plains.

Here, the vagabond's odyssey takes a gradual turn into the bittersweetness of the holiday season—as well as the early stages of a good father's rapid decline— as the astronomical year winds down to its longest night. Yet another beginning to a couple of looming endings. Endings that will have to find their way through to another beginning of a new year.

*This book is dedicated
to the beautiful memory of
my extraordinary parents*

*Norma
and
Lavonn
Brown*

*   *   *

And I must thank my dear friends:
Konrad Eek, who helped create the
reproductions of the mandalas that
appear in the next-to-last chapter; and
my spiritual brother and guide, Chris
Everett, who created the graphic design
work for the covers in this series.

Autumn
is a distance you see in
certain trees,

~ Steven Schroeder
"News from Other Mountains"

*   *   *

Where are the songs of Spring?
Ay, where are they?
Think not of them, thou hast
thy music too,—

~ John Keats
"To Autumn"

The
Fallen
Autumn

Nathan Brown

~ SEPTEMBER ~

An Odd Season

September 23

Autumn coasted in around 2:50 a.m.
Greenwich Mean Time, if I want to get
all technical about it. But I don't. I woke
up at 6:35, which is close enough for me,
and was on the road when the sun rose
behind me on Highway 9 in Oklahoma.

A few hours before the equinox, I had
been sitting on a bench at the end of a
wooden dock that juts out 50 feet into
Shawnee Lake, staring at the rippled
reflection of a near-half Harvest Moon.
The evening's house concert—a lovely
affair on a big back porch overlooking
the water—was long over. But a group
of people were still going at it up there,
dimly lit under the spinning of outdoor
ceiling fans. I saw it as a sign that I had

done my job. They were talking about music, politics, and even poetry…a little.

I used a text from Ashley as a way to bow out of the conversation and made my dark escape down to the dock. I was needing to be alone with my hot stew of mismatched thoughts—one part feeling good about how the concert had gone, but another part the little gut-bomb that goes off every time I gear up to point the car back toward Texas.

Yet another ingredient in the mix—that both sweetened and soured the pot— had to do with the onset of Autumn. I capitalized it, I guess, because it is, and has always been, my favorite season of the year. And in all the years Ashley and I spent together, it was ours as well.

We looked forward to the equinox. We couldn't wait for that first pumpkin— usually bought on October 1st. We got excited about fires glowing in my stone castles. Thanksgiving and Christmas were always so important to both our families. But now, stirred in with all that anticipation, brews the underlying dread of "What about this year?" All the who, and who not; the where, and where not; the when, and when not—as well as the nagging inevitabilities that will arise in decision making.

To be blunt, I went through decades of this with my daughter, and, selfishly, I'd hoped to never have to go through it again. But I'm not a special case—as life likes to remind me…on a regular basis. And so, my guess is that these next few months will test my grand scheme and big talk around saying Yes to everything.

Ah, but hell, I'll jump off those bridges when I get to each one. For now, I'm sailing down I-35 to join Ashley and a small group of friends around my fire pit, where we'll burn away our troubles beneath the next slightly bigger slice of that Harvest Moon, and then we'll usher in this odd and unknowable version of the best season.

The Fire of Fall

September 24

They each one arrived with their own heartaches and lovebreaks, for a wide variety of reasons, to join our aches and breaks in celebration of the fall equinox that marks Persephone's return to the underworld—a mythical remembrance that makes our problems look paltry by comparison.

I had asked everyone to write out on paper something they wanted to let go of and bring it with them to the fire pit. First, of course, we shook up cocktails and shared food in our own little pagan communion. But then, we made our way out to my sacred medicine space with our drinks and all the things we wanted to let go of.

I kept the fire small, since the afternoon had crept up—once again—to over 100 degrees. This time of year, though, when the sun bows down in the west, the heat eases off pretty quickly. Besides, I've lost my ability to respect, or care about, the damnable heat of Texas. I was going to have this shindig—this welcoming of Autumn—and the angry sun could just kiss my bare ass (which it is known to do, when I work out among the stones without any clothes on. It happens.)

Most of us were letting go of fear— tossing into the fire our concerns about things not working out, people letting us down…uncertainties about our families, finances, and health issues, et al.

For one, it was her fear for the future in general. For another, the plight of our planet. And two of us chose not to read what we'd written, but very thoughtfully and deliberately placed it in the flames. Two silences not lost on the others.

A respectful quiet descended—a soft reverence that firelight always seems to command. Catharsis hovered in the air around it. And our fears…for now… turned to ashes before our eyes.

So, the hurts and losses, whether spoken
out loud or not, lost a little of their fever
and fury. And we breathed lighter air—
for a time, at least.

The moon, though blazing, remained
hushed along with us, offering just the
right amount of light. And it felt like fall
might have a chance yet, in the slow drift
of this unanchored year.

Baring It All

September 25

It was a small act, a simple gesture toward some greater need, that I committed when I woke up this morning— just as the sun opened its eye on the lid of the eastern horizon.

I stepped back out to the fire pit at that sacred and fleeting time of day when the early light sets the limestone walls ablaze in a shock of bright orange and yellow. They become a fire unto themselves at this liminal threshold, when a soul that's awake enough can see more clearly that the stones are alive—that they're just as animate as you and I, their faces so full of expression.

The difference this morning, though, was that I stepped out there barefooted. I know…seems like nothing. But what made it something—an unusual thing— was that I don't recall ever having done it. My sad soles prissed at the pokes of

grass, small rocks, and the cedar mulch.
It's where the term "tenderfoot" comes
from. And it ain't a compliment.

I made it out to the center of the circle,
letting the Earth speak to my shy feet.
She was as kind as she could be. Yet…
also a little reprimanding, and with a bit
of a snarky undertone of: *Well, it took ya'
long enough.* I winced. I felt humbled—
apologetic even.

Over the years together, I never fully
understood Ashley's feelings—or rules
maybe? or was it a phobia?—about bare
feet. But something was going on there.
She does not want them indoors, for
some reason. But she doesn't care for
them outdoors either. It's something to
do with getting them dirty. And she may
disagree on certain points, or all. But I
felt uncomfortable and self-conscious,
nonetheless. And this is my book.

For the record, it contributed very little
to the breakup. But…here I am, now,
barefooted, as I write up in the garage

apartment. Not as an act of defiance…
just a simple gesture, as I said, intended
as a symbol of returning to myself. To a
thing I did every day as a young buck in
Oklahoma. But also, if not more so, it
reconnects me to the Earth. The warm
dirt we eventually return to.

So, in the wake of marital separation
(that I now see as a severance), I am
determined to end, and to repair, the
other separations in my life. Or at least
as many as I can. And that list includes,
along with a few other things I'll think
of later: separations from my self, my
soul, my heart, air, water, soil, spirit, the
stones, ceremony, certain friends, and
the road. As well as the flâneur in me.

And it begins here, with a little bit of dirt
between my bare toes.

Poco Dinero

Nothing uncomplicates life and the future more than removing money from the concerns you have about both.

I have written before about my growing awareness that I am not an "owner." At my core, I'm more of a "renter" at best. Though I suppose I'm mostly prone to wander. A "passer-througher" of sorts.

Whatever we go with, it reminds me of one of my favorite John Gorka lines in his song, "The Gypsy Life"—

> People love you when they
> know you're leaving soon

A less funny few lines, from later in the same song, say:

> If you choose to settle
>   in one place
> You may be harder over

> on the ones you love
> Like a tree without
> the growing space
> You will be taking from below
> and from above

But those are larger concerns about life and how, or maybe where, to live it. And when it comes to the future, I don't see this part of who I am changing any time soon. But, I meant to talk about money and how it factors into all of that.

Some believe the way to remove all concerns about money is to (as Garth Brooks admitted once) have more than your grandkids would ever be able to spend. Not a problem I'm likely to have. But what I have witnessed, in the people who try to achieve that goal, is the self-defeating side effect of: the more they make, the more they obsess over how to hold onto it, as well as stress over who's scheming to get a piece of it. And they don't seem to enjoy the obsession, nor the stress. And, ergo, the money itself.

At the other end of the stick, for as long as I've been old enough to have money (in my pocket or the bank), I've never felt I have as much as I need. Despite the times I've quoted Jesus or romanticcized the lives of hermits, for most of my working life I have worried about getting by. And also what others think about my lack of income and a 401K.

So here in this time of losing so much and letting go of even more, as I near the age of 60, I'm struck by what should be an obvious truth: I have *always* gotten by. When things get slim? I go without. When there's a little extra? I treat myself. And, if there's a little bit on top of that? I put it back for when things get *too* slim. Six decades of this. To which I ask the question: *Why would the next two or three be any different?*

Look…I do what I do. I make what I make. I'll die when I die. And I'll die of what I die of when time runs out. And if the money runs out before then? Well… maybe I'll die of that.

In the Void

September 27

All Japhy's doing is amusing
himself in the void.

~ Ray Smith

RockHaus Coffee in Fredericksburg,
Texas has four small marble-top tables
in a tiny front room on the main drag.
It's a cozy spot for reading Kerouac's
The Dharma Bums, if you can score a seat.
And I did. And so far, Ray Smith—who
is Kerouac not even thinly disguised—is
a bit whiny for my tastes. As well as too
cock sure about too many things. But,
I'm only on page 50. So I'll give him
some more time to win me over.

Fredericksburg is a tourist town with a
German problem. Or, maybe I should
say, it's a German town with a tourist
problem. Either way, the big sign on the
way in shouts: "WILLKOMMEN" at you.
A welcome meaning "received with

gladness." Which is funny, in the sense that a word that means such a friendly thing, can still manage to *sound* angry, somehow. Like the word for Hello in Russian: Zdravstvuyte—which has a miraculous arrangement of consonants and is one of the hardest words in the language to learn how to pronounce, properly.

Even though we lived close for years, Ashley and I never quite caught onto this popular Hill Country destination. It appears mostly to be a long pair of wide sidewalks for beer-drinkers and bleach-blonds to walk up and down in shorts and skirts and oversized t-shirts while they shop for Texas chintz or German schlock between pitstops at biergartens. Which, of course, is a grossly superficial take on what might be an honest town. I'm just telling you what I've seen in the years of passing through here—and, occasionally, stopping. But I bet you can get a mean kolache along this strip.

Fire and Buzz

When you wake up, roll over, then try to stand, and your breathing stops from a flashfire of pain shooting to your brain from your lower back, so you sink back to the bed because your only option is to fall to the floor…your first thought is:

> *Okay…the show is six hours away.*
> *So, we gotta get there somehow, buddy.*
> *Because the sweet hostess has whipped*
> *up a ranch-spread of food laced with*
> *every type of meat known to Texas,*
> *and their guests have all RSVPed.*

So you gather your mental gonads, go for it again, and suck down the electro-chemical firestorm blazing across your synaptic gaps. You grab the dresser and pull your left foot forward, but the right one refuses. It's just too much. So, you stand there a while, beginning to sweat from this tiny bit of effort, and you look around for help that's not coming. Thus, your second thought is: *This is bad.*

Time seems to do some good, in microscopic increments. You make it to the bathroom. And what happens in there, regarding the toilet, is not a story that's gonna get told here. But then, you pop an ibuprofen afterwards and drag your right leg to the kitchen. Over more time, you begin to figure out what movements do and do not work. Then, you look at the guitar, your bags, and those book boxes in the floor, and realize they are going to have to make it down the stairs and into the car. Another pause.

It's 8:30-ish now. Ashley won't be up for an hour or more over in the big house. And you're not gonna call—because you are not together anymore, and you're a stubborn-ass fool. So you refuse to even consider it.

First, however, a shower has to be had somehow. Which does, because it's an upright situation—though quite painful nonetheless. But all this leads to is the need to get dressed. Which is going to be more near to impossible than you realize. And yet, through a weird series of footstools, chairs, and an Ottoman, you get it done—with a few screams interspersed. It takes about 20 minutes too. Which brings you to your third thought, that's really a question:

> *So how long is it going to take to load the car? Holy crap.*

Fast forward. There's no way to explain the series of draggings down stairs that took place, followed by contorted acts of leverage. Let's just say it got done. But it took so long, Ashley was now up and bringing Lacey out for a morning walk. That's when she saw me leaning against the car, gasping, and almost in tears.

She cared. Which is her way, no matter what—with all animals…as well as with some varieties of humans. She handed me Lacey's leash and went back inside to retrieve her TENS device to hook me up

to. But, Lacey was not happy her walk
was being delayed and lunged in Ashley's
direction, sending me into paroxysms of
spinal shock. I fell against the car door,
moaned, and waited.

When she got back, she surrounded the
ground zero of my lower back with two
pairs of sticky electrodes that she then
plugged into a little black box. (A fairly
unnerving sight.) She turned it on and
slowly cranked up the amps. I felt a tiny
tingling. She paused, then bumped it up
to quite a bit more tingle.

Now…I'm not sure about the healing
properties of thingamajiggers like this?
However, it *was* rather warm and buzzy.
Very buzzy. So it distracted me enough
to help me maneuver into my car. And
then, I buzzed off in the direction of
Crowell, Texas, where I had a concert to
play at a ranch outside of town—about
six buzzy hours away.

Oh What a Night

September 30

About eight miles west of Crowell (pro-
nounced "Crow'll"), on Highway 70 in
Foard County, Texas, is not a part of
North America everyone's going to see.
And anyone who believes urban streets
are canyons made of concrete, and that
rooftops constitute a horizon, or that car
horns are nature's soundtrack to life…
may not want to. But they'd be missing
some inexplicable thing—a desolate, yet
living, mythology. Like the sight of iron-
red dirt and gold tallgrass rolling off to
faraway flattop hills and those evermore
distant medicine mounds. The sound of
a lonely south wind rattling dried-up oak
leaves. The perfume of roasting asphalt
and donkey shit. And the hard shock of
a mesquite or cactus needle—or, maybe
a rattlesnake's tooth.

Ah, but I should add in the taste of
bacon-wrapped quail sausages, deep-
fried jalapeño-cheese poppers, Pigs-

21

in-a-Blanket Little Smokies wrapped in
crescent roll dough. And don't leave out
the Armadillo Eggs: a hot jalapeño filled
with cream cheese that's stuffed inside a
big ball of breakfast sausage, and then,
lovingly placed into a Traeger Smoker
out back, until done to perfection.

And that wasn't half the spread laid out
for concertgoers in this beautiful ranch
house. Add to it wine, beer, and margaritas made with fine añejo tequila, along
with a 600-milligram prescription-grade
ibuprofen offered me by the kind host,
and I'll tell ya', come showtime? I was
ready to rock *and* roll, bad back and all.
I weren't feelin' *no* pain. And weren't
nobody else feelin' theirs neither…
hallelujah, thank ya' Lord, and Frankie
Valli and the Four Seasons…

> *Oh what a night*
> *Late September back in '23*
> *What a very special time for me*
> *As I remember, what a night*

(Sing it with me!)

~ OCTOBER ~

The Dying of the Light

October 1

I bought Ashley a small pumpkin—an Orange Sparkler, according to the tiny barcode sticker—with deep ridges and an unusually long and thin stem. Only on the drive home did I notice how phallic it looked. Oh well…today is October 1st. And some fifteen-year-old habits are hard to break—little gestures that remind us there were, and are, good things between us.

This day excites me because it's still so "front edge" to my belovéd Autumn. Still early enough in the season that I have not started, yet, to worry that it's going to end—a waste of time I'm prone to. So, the day had to be marked in some way. And an Orange Sparkler pumpkin, though cute, was not enough.

The other plan was to build a ceremonial fire at dusk and sit with it as long as my back would last. It had been the worst day yet. So I knew what pain awaited me in gathering up the kindling and bending over far enough to try and light it. But, some things have to be done.

The evening felt perfect for it—a tad warm, but not hot, for a change. And, that would only improve as the sun got lower. The air sat still. The stars fired up their engines. I growled with every cedar twig I picked up. I groaned as I knelt to light it, and gasped as I got back up. The good thing, though?—you never have to light dry cedar twice. It takes. It's the jet fuel of firewoods.

From there on, adding to it didn't hurt as much. I have tall stacks of that stuff. So I took my seat. I rubbed the gentle curves of my margarita, just below her salty rim, took a sip now and then, and watched the flames blossom.

GoldenHeart had suggested I bring the Blue Heron feather and a small piece of obsidian she'd given me out to the fire, for healing energy, and said that she'd be sending some my way as well. They sat, reverently, next to the añejo margarita. A trifecta of sacred ingredients.

Soon, the quiet softly announced its presence. It married the lick and roll of the flames. I became transfixed. Time gave up its nagging insistence. I was breathing now. More like you're supposed to. More deeply and consciously.

Then, the waning Harvest Moon rose over the eastern stone walls through a scraggly oak—a bit overripe…but still full of milk and burning bright. I tilted my head back to take in my dark home, The Sky. And it hit me that, because of that sky, this particular space—the Fire Circle—will always belong to me. I don't have to let it go—as I was sure I would, back in the Broken Summer. Even if I'm not able to physically visit, eventually, for some reason, there'll be no way to exorcise my soul from what I've created here—nor from the spirit of the beautiful things that occurred in its sphere.

When the moon peaked, and I relaxed into it, at that very moment a ghost bird swooshed straight over my head from behind—so close I heard the air in its wing and tail feathers. It swooped back up and disappeared through the cedars before me into the darkness beyond.

Immediately, I recalled the haunting bird that had risen, Christlike, from the piñon trees up on the summit of Cerro Gordo, come to release me from the mountain. This bird looked somewhat similar, in both appearance and the way in which it rose up and flew off. So, I wondered if I was being followed.

That's when I felt the first tremor run through me. Which brought on the full quaking. The blood began to simmer in my veins as I watched smoke from the fire rise above my head—just like that bird into the darkness. Tears began to roll down my temples into my ears. My chest began to heave in pulsing waves. And then…I erupted into sobs. Sobs occasionally interrupted by wails and moans. Wordless prayers offered up to the night dome.

I can't say how long this went on. But, when my head came to upright, the fire was mostly coals. I picked up the Blue Heron feather and rolled it between my thumb and forefinger. I took a sip of margarita, then set it down to grab the piece of obsidian with the other hand.

I took a turn looking at each, then lifted my gaze up to the deep-red coals. And, that's when, in my mind's eye, the third eye, I saw my former life—whoever it was I thought or believed I'd been in this marriage—dissolve into that dim and dying light.

The Angel of My Pain

October 2

As my lower back will likely be a main character in the story of the trip out to Oregon later this week, I should also acknowledge the angel who—if I indeed survive the flight—will have been the gifted guardian who made it possible.

After making it to Crowell, and then barely back again, by the skin of my gritting teeth, I woke up the following morning in the same frying pan of pain, but with the heat turned up a notch. So, I began to have visions of what security at the airport, and the overhead bins on the plane, were going to be like. Untying my shoes, taking them off, putting them back on and retying them, would be a melodramatic moment that would likely frighten smaller children. And lifting a suitcase full of clothes and books over my head would simply be a no-can-do.

In desperation, I texted my therapist—
who has a few sports medicine contacts
through the University of Texas—to
plead my case. And despite my having
graduated from their nemesis university
up in Oklahoma—a point of contention
more serious than coastal folks might
think—he put me in direct contact with
a buddy who's a first-rate chiropractor.

To my surprise, he got right back to me.
(Keep in mind it was Sunday afternoon.)
There was no opening until Wednesday.
I reeled, because I leave for the airport at
5:45 a.m. on Thursday. So, he offered to
take me on his lunchbreak on Monday.
The first sign of a saint.

In my experience with humans, it would
be tough to find a nicer guy than Dr.
Daniel Bockmann. He ushered me in
with a bright smile and what looked to
be a very straight and healthy back. He
listened to me for almost 30 minutes,
before going to work on my problem.

And then, when he did, I must say: no one has ever hurt me more gently and politely, nor with more care and good intention. He took me through motions I wouldn't have thought possible in my condition. He sent me an email, as we spoke, with exercises I could do at home (one involving a used softball I bought at Play It Again Sports right after the session). It included YouTube videos of him demonstrating them. And, also…he prescribed no medications. I mean, what doctor doesn't do that? Well, okay…he did mention THC? Quietly? But, really, who wouldn't—off the record?

I still hurt when I left. But I had some amount of hope for Oregon now. It *seemed* like I might be able to get my shoes off and back on at security.

And this brings me to the reason I bothered to write this story. Because it must be said. Dan Bockmann—the man, not the doctor—has Stage Four cancer, and roughly two to six months to live.

The man gave up his lunch break to help me. He was upbeat the entire hour and fifteen minutes. He never spoke of his own pain, only mine. He gave me tips to make my life better in the long run, not just my back. And so, you now see the reason I called him an angel in the first paragraph.

I'm not only feeling better, I'm humbled by such a raw goodness…such a kind toughness…and such a healing spirit in one being visited by other, darker angels.

And he should be remembered for it.

Miracles and Thunders

October 3

Standing up out of bed hurt a bit less
this morning. But, doing it at 5:25 a.m.
to an audience of darkness, thunder, and
a pouring rain, hurt in a different kind of
way. The weather would slow the drive
on the shoulderless two-lanes between
here and the airport. So I needed to get
on past the grunts and groans of putting
clothes on and load the car, again.

I pulled out into the falling sky, and
within minutes, the guy on KUT—
Austin's NPR station—said: *Well, folks,
bad news for those of you who have flights to
catch this morning. All lanes of 71 are shut
down at Spirit of Texas Drive, due to a crash.*

And I thought, *Likely due to the fact that
Central Texans don't know how to drive in
rain anymore—due to the fact that it doesn't
rain here anymore—except on the one morning
I need to get to the airport.*

When I got close, an hour later, I'm not sure how to explain what happened. I spotted the symphony of red and blue flashing lights up ahead in the very early dawn. But, the early exit for the parking service I use, though crowded, was still working. And the left lane I needed to turn from was clear. So, in a couple of minutes, I was parked in slot N28, and a minibus whisked me off. The nice driver threaded the traffic, at one point using a small side road I never knew existed, and then dumped me off at the curb about fifteen minutes earlier than I'd had the slightest hope of arriving.

Only in Austin would they park a food truck indoors—a real perk of Bergstrom International Airport. It's a nice place to grab a breakfast taco and contemplate minor travel miracles over scrambled eggs and coffee. I sat at a table next to the big live music stage decked out to the max with lighting and sound gear—

yet another thing only the Austin airport would do. (Of course, I don't know that for sure. But it seems plausible.)

And yet, as luck would have it, no live band was rockin' out with bad tattoos and distorted steel guitars this morning. Likely because Austin musicians can't function until 3:00 p.m. or later. They need time for the caffeine and THC to hit their systems after waking up. So, their absence, as twilight turned to light gray, was a blessing. Yet another minor miracle. No offence to my friends in the business. It's just too early in the day for Americana angst.

I had a champion snorer over by the window who availed me of his skill all the way to Las Vegas. To balance it out, though, we had the only open seat on a "full flight" between us. A slightly more major miracle—one that I will take *every*

time. Because unfamiliar elbows rub me the wrong way.

Across the aisle, I had a guy with two smartphones glowing on his tray-table, each one tuned to a different NFL game. Thank god he didn't have the sound up on either one. And if it had been both at once, there would've been an altercation.

After an hour and a half or so of mild turbulence and snoring, we began a smooth descent. That's when my window friend came to and began to talk. He'd been a police officer in San Diego after leaving the military, until a scuffle with a guy on PCP screwed up his back beyond repair. He'd noticed my jerky movements and vocal squeaks of pain and told me I needed to track down some mangosteen juice. It's an exotic fruit from south Asia that hasn't been approved over here yet, but you can get the goods online. *And make sure*, he said, *you get it unpasteurized. The stuff is super anti-inflammatory.*

Since he couldn't police anymore, he
became a pastor and author of mostly
nonfiction to do with God. Ah, but his
lovechild is his barbecue sauce company
he started, that offers twelve different
variations—his very own creations. He
gave me a card. (Looks like tasty stuff.)
And he turned out to be a good guy. So
I feel bad about my snoring comments.

If Bergstrom International is all about
food trucks, breakfast tacos, and live
music, Harry Reid International in Las
Vegas is all slot machines: Buffalo Gold,
Cashman Bingo, or Wheel of Fortune.
Whatever steals your coin.

Personally? I'd rather lose money on
tacos, coffee, and tequila. That's why—
after the flight for Eugene took off, and
we drifted past the MGM Grand, the
Paris (where Ashley and I had stayed
when I was finishing my book *Letters to
the One-Armed Poet*), then Treasure Island

and the Mirage, which were followed by
the obscenity of a lush green golf course
in the middle of a hot desert, which then
eventually turned into the bone-dry dirt
and gray-brown stones up in the Sheep
Mountain Range—I ordered an O.J. and
tequila to have me a little sunrise in the
middle of the afternoon.

I mean, why should every day have just
one? Besides, it is my unscientific theory
that tequila kills Covid dead in its tracks.
I'll let you know if it works…again. I've
been collecting data in support of this
theory since the pandemic began. Well,
in all honesty, since long before then.
It's just that I believe tequila cures about
every ailment there is—physical, mental,
or otherwise. To go with that, it helps
me relax after a long day of being forced
into near proximity with hundreds, really
thousands, of other human beings—a
thing I can only take for limited periods
of time. Though…I love people.

No…really…I do.

Could Be Worse

October 4

I woke up to a purple-dawn view of the Siuslaw River in Florence, Oregon. And, just beyond the jetty on the far side of it, I now have a clear shot of a long cobalt sliver of the Pacific Ocean from the back porch, where I'm writing.

Fishing boats are heading out in a steady stream to where the river's mouth meets the largest body of water on earth in a gentle curve—an ancient marriage…till death do them part.

In a small cove of the river, directly below me, harbor seals are lolling around in the dark waters that would freeze my ass off. And it has me thinking of how seldom my landlocked southern self gets to use words like *jetty* and *ocean*, or *seal* and *freeze*. And I wonder if I shouldn't work to cure that sadness before too long. I am a Pisces, after all.

Anyway, as the sun rises higher and hits the lovely array of plants and flowers my friends have planted along the back line of their yard that overlooks all of this, and I catch sight of a pelican (another word I don't get to use enough) gliding just above the water, I'm doing my best to take the whole scene in, with the awe it is due.

Just as Jockomo, the very sweet and very black Australian Labradoodle sitting beside me, is doing a better job of.

And I think to myself: *You know? I have been in much worse situations. Quite a few, in fact. This year alone, so far.*

Finding the Mean

October 5

It's 80-something-some-odd degrees in coastal Oregon in early October, and everyone here is talking Apocalypse.

So far, I've held back my bursts of laughter bubbling up from the lower bowels of the hell I just left behind in Texas. But I doubt it will last long.

I suppose most people sort of get into the meteorological rhythm of wherever they happen to live. Or, like me, they do not. The bottom of the middle of Texas can be nice, sometimes, roughly four to six months out of the year—namely, the four to six with the least amount of daylight. Otherwise, it's ice storms or heat waves. And the heat waves rule.

Here in Florence, I am told the mean annual temperature is around 55°. The all-knowing Internet says it typically varies between 41° to 67° and is rarely below 33° or above 71°. My god. Are you kidding me? If a snarky friend in Texas—who is soon to not be a friend anymore, because I'm heading to the northwest—were to ask me: *Well, what would you prefer for weather, ya' little pansy?* (because he loves the heat), I'd answer: *Well, ya' asshole, about 41° to 67° year-round would do.*

That said, the average temperature here inside Tsunami Books over in Eugene, with all the doors wide open—where I played some songs and read poetry with a dear friend, Beth Wood, to a small but appreciative crowd—felt pretty close to perfect.

Living in the Flow

October 7

Yesterday morning, before heading out to Sisters, my friends in Florence took me to the beach south of Dunes City, where the Siltcoos River winds its way into the ocean. They say it often changes in shape and direction, because storms and the tides are always moving the sand of its banks around. This is where the Council of Great Waters meets. And winter storms can be fierce and brutal.

There's a little bit of beach on the inland side of the river. Then across the river there is a lot more beach over to the crashing waves—a flat area between large grassy sand dunes. The dunes are epic here. Mountainous. So every other vehicle that comes into the park has a four-wheel dune buggy on a flatbed. Because leaving the pristine beauty and quiet of creation unscathed by tire marks and gas fumes would be silly—as well as a waste of good deep-drilled petroleum.

We didn't have to deal with them, though, since where we were walking was flat and boring. So all I could hear was that Precambrian song of the moon-licked crests ever falling into each other. Which did to me what it always does to me: it reminds me that I am a fish. That I live under its sign. And I need to take that more seriously. That eternal roar mesmerizes me. I can sit in its presence for hours, without moving or feeling a need to do something more productive.

Later that morning, heading east out of Eugene, I followed the McKenzie River for about an hour. And for the first 30 minutes or more, it's a wide and dark, very full and lusciously flowing thing—immense and powerful. It reminds me that what we call rivers in Texas are just oversized bar ditches made of limestone that seldom flow, but do occasionally have small stagnant pools full of algae.

Nimrod doesn't appear all that biblical in scale, but I did notice a wooden sign for Heaven's Gate River Cabins on the far side of this tiny town. Yes, it's a rather unfortunate choice of names. But, the folks out here may not worry that much about cults and mass suicides that took place at the bottom of the long golden state below them. So far away.

What hurts to see up here are the blackened bases of the huge Douglas Firs on both sides of the road. So many of them dead and gray toothpicks now. Some of them have tried to hang on, though, with patches of green poking out from straggles of limbs. One in particular looked dead most of the way up. But then, at about 60 to 70 feet high, what looked like a perfect Christmas tree levitated above the graveyard below, like an evergreen angel ascending into the heavens.

Deeper into the Willamette National Forest, the lush hunter green returned. And in this nation of the living, I pulled off the road to hike down to Koosah Falls. Here the massive conifers swallow you whole, and you can hear the chorus of the falls from the top of the trail.

As the crystal-blue cascade came into view through the drooping boughs, I caught myself looking around for trees full of forbidden fruit and a big snake— maybe even a woman wearing nothing but fig leaves. Like Adam, I'm such a sucker. I would bite into it too.

Every time I have experiences like this, I always feel sorry for people who have somewhere they believe they've got to be. I'd bet there are folks who live on Highway 126 who've never stopped in to see this magnificent waterfall. Or, just as important to me, hear it. That sound is a Siren calling me to come and join the pool party that never ends. Because the water is that fine.

I sat for a long spell listening to this deep pulsation in one of the Earth's veins. A pure liquid meditation. Tears came. But I'm getting used to that on this journey. And, remember, Odysseus was a much bigger crybaby than I am. At least I don't wail and pound my fists on the sand in front of Calypso's beach house, for God's sake.

No, these were quiet tears, as I thought back to the morning's walk by the ocean, then the beauty of the silent flowing of the McKenzie River on the drive, and now...this angelic chorus.

That's when the message began to form, as if an old Chinese hermit had stepped

out of his mountain cave with a cup of
wine and a devious smile to deliver the
one sentence that would change my life
forever:

> If you are a fish…if your sign lives
> in water, my son…you can't keep
> living in a blazing hot dead-zone
> that is soon to be a desert made of
> drought, wind, and fire.

Oh God, Oh God, Oh God

October 8

Of course it would be when you're 2,000 miles from home, staying with the kind parents of a friend, that you would wake up in the middle of the night muttering, *Oh God, oh God, oh God*, because you feel it coming on—the sore throat, stopped-up nose, and the body aches.

Your first thought is: Covid…from the airplane—because where else would you get it from. Your second thought is that you are now the Grim Reaper, delivering death to all the good people of Oregon. And your third thought is that you can no longer distinguish between the back pain and these new crud-related aches coursing through your body.

So, when you drag yourself up in the wee hours of the night to trudge to the bathroom, you experience a wild orgy of dull throbs and sharp twinges that make it difficult to stand up from the toilet when you're done. But then, also, quite problematic to try and lie back down in bed again—a lose-lose situation.

And this brings you to your fourth thought: *Oh God. I have to play a house concert tomorrow night, and then teach a workshop at the bookstore the following day.*

So you fumble around in your suitcase for the ibuprofen PM, mumble your way back between the sheets, and spend the rest of the night alternating between shivers and sweats—and occasionally muttering, *Oh God, oh God, oh God.*

The Show Goes On

October 9

When I woke up in the morning, I felt like a good old dog on the day he's been scheduled to be put down—sad to leave the world, and yet, it's probably best for everyone involved.

But, since that was not going to happen, I had to work my way up to a standing position, then try to figure out what the hell to do from there. When I spoke out loud to myself about my options—as I'm prone to do—I noticed my voice had dropped an octave. So I immediately thought about the evening's concert and, this time, just said a single, *Oh god.*

The first order of business would be to get down to Oliver Lemon's "Not Your Usual Market" to buy some bone broth and Throat Coat tea. Most everything in Sisters is only a few blocks away. So that would be manageable.

Next, I'd have to figure out how to not talk to anybody all day without coming across as a jerk. Both of which are hard for me: not talking, and not coming across as a jerk. But I am working on them. And I accomplished each one by going to a coffee shop and writing most of the afternoon, then going back to take a nap, followed by an irresponsibly long, hot shower.

The "venue" for the night's show was a gorgeous front yard just outside of town on five acres. The "stage" was a Persian throw-rug with a chair and a big slice of pine trunk for an end table. Between two trees, over to my left, was a 50-foot long, inexplicably artistic stack of firewood for the winter. And though I couldn't even imagine Dennis burning all that beauty, I know he will. He has to.

With some vocal exercises and a fresh margarita, I tried to jumpstart my voice.

And I worried about my odds. But then, as always seems to happen, I somehow croaked out a whole set of poems and songs—my voice waiting until the last note to give out. Everyone was quite forgiving, as well as generous with the donation jar. One enthusiastic listener said: *This collection of the Pandemic Poems Project should be in the Smithsonian!* Then, she and several others suggested that I should move to Sisters. And I told them I would seriously consider their offer.

We all lingered over a ridiculous spread of finger foods. I patched my margarita. And, while my body remained broken, my soul revived—just enough for me to make the dark drive back to yet another ibuprofen PM and a warm bed.

Downriver

Dennis, who's front yard I'd played in, told me about a new human subspecies he'd been spotting lately. He calls them the Subaru Haters: local guys—because, males are the most problematic half of all species—in big pickups who harass and ride the asses of Subarus, because they represent the opposition to a carte blanche American freedom to shoot liberal neighbors with assault rifles and destroy the planet with their black-smoke-billowing exhaust pipes.

Have I mentioned that the car my awesome friends in Florence have loaned me is a practically-new white Subaru Crosstrek? So just know, I'm keeping my eyes peeled as I head back downriver to the coast.

The news of that came about the same time I began to hear hints on the radio that Armageddon may have finally be-

gun over in Israel. Yes, Hell hath finally
arrived…on the wings of hang gliders
and unguided solid-propellant rockets.
Murder, mayhem, hostage-taking, and
the massacring of children at a music
festival in the Negev Desert.

I don't pay much attention to the news
anymore—but doubly so when I travel.
It calms me. And I pay better attention
to the road. But that old classic headline
buzzword "unprecedented" is hanging in
the air, once again, like a nighttime flare
hovering in the desert sky.

So, I give up and give in to the public
radio chatter about it. I reflect on the
Subaru Haters, and it hits me like a
missile strike: Only men. Only men
dream up wars. Well, men…and the
goddess Athena. And look, I'm aware
there are female suicide bombers. And I
also know a few ladies who likely hate
Subarus. But, when it comes to large-
scale destruction and death, and the
slaughter of innocents, I would bet
you…99 to 1…men are behind it.

This news from Israel hurts me on many
levels. One is that I have traveled there,
several times back in the 1980s and 90s.
And I am just now recalling a long and
sultry drive past the Dead Sea, through
the baking sands of the Negev, and then
down to the southernmost city of Eilat
on the northern tip of the Red Sea.

At a food stand along the boardwalk
there, a beautiful young woman with
long black hair, and a kill-you smile,
brought me a falafel sandwich I had
ordered while some silly 80s love song
was playing on the kitchen radio. I sang
it to her—under my breath. And she
seemed the type who would attend a
music festival. So, I am allowing for a
few tears this morning, here at River
Roasters coffee shop by the bridge in
Florence, as a gray rain falls into the
Siuslaw—the dark river that will carry
that rain, and my tears, to the sea.

Dancing Around It

October 11

Famous men of letters cast heavy artistic shadows over their children who pursue their own dreams in their own forms and genres. It's hard for people to see the gifts of the new for the awards and prizes of the old. And the same is likely true for famous women of letters—as well as famous men and women in all the arts—but I don't know any of their children. I only know two gifted children of two famous men of letters. At least that I know of.

Maybe I should mention that both these artists I'm referring to as children are older than me. Or maybe I shouldn't. Maybe it doesn't matter. But, one tells me she loved her father. He was a great dad. The other I do believe loved his father—if love is the word. But he's not likely to talk about it.

To compare and contrast the quality or mastery of the work of these four artists would be as irresponsible as it would be useless. But know that the long, heavy shadows of the formers do not make the lives and endeavors of the latters any easier. If anything, they complicate the process of self-actualization. Yes, it's a Gordian Knot of a game, best I can tell. But I cannot speak with authority. My father didn't win the Pulitzer. Though my father is a great man.

Anyway, I met one of those two "kids" for coffee in a cozy mountain town in Oregon yesterday—a town I now want to move to (for more reasons than just her) and she read me a wonderful new poem she'd just written. And it was alive with dancing language—because she's a dancer, as well as a poet. And while her father was a fine poet, he was not a dancer that I know of. Which, as far as I'm concerned, makes her a little bit *more* of something I cannot explain.

Some New World

If you don't know where to pull over on the 101, you'll easily miss it—the hidden portal to Middle-earth. But, somewhere over on the watery side of the road is the entrance to the Hobbit Trail—a dark, serpentine path through a fog-riddled forest made of black trunks and gnarled limbs covered in a deep velvety-green moss. Parts of it are practically tunnels made of mud walls, and with a roof of densely-braided sea brush. The floor is a tangle of toothy roots that seem to snap at you to trip you up. But the sun shoots thin rays through holes in the fog just often enough to coax you on.

And then, after a sharp curve to the left, through a sandy wormhole, you emerge onto the shore of the Sundering Seas in the heart of Endor. Where, by the way, I happened to see an unusually large set of bare footprints?

Nearby, a rivulet of fresh water—
formed by numerous trickles gurgling
out of the thick weeds and sand of the
hillside, like blood out of the side of
Christ—cut its own winding path down
to the beach in search of its great salty
mentor. It reminded me how the trees
were dripping back in the woods, even
though it was not raining. The tangles of
roots glistened, wet as a dog running up
out of a river. The air itself was liquid,
like a hysterical nation of two-to-one
hydrogen and oxygen molecules, all
commuting to work in the morning—
every one of them dreaming of the sea.

It turns out, those small rivulets are
everywhere up and down this hidden
beach. Because here at the end-point in
their journey, rivers just are not enough
to contain the water's joy. It spurts and
it springs from the earth, draining down
cliff edges and falling from exposed
roots.

On the receiving end, the ocean storms
the beach in a wild rush of spindrift and

foamy love, crying its saline tears for the
reunion with its freshwater aunts, uncles,
and cousins.

And, standing at the convergence of this
festival drenched in desire, the blood in
my veins began to celebrate with the
masses. It felt as if I were being wel-
comed into an ancient order of the
marine world that only reveals itself to
humans born under the sign of Pisces.
Any minute, I thought Poseidon, that
old angry Greek, might rise just off the
shore and tap each of my shoulders with
his brass Trident.

But then I remembered I'd come down
on the Hobbit Trail. That's a different
mythscape altogether. But, it did not
matter to me. I was wandering in my
own Narnia now.

No, wait. That's C.S. Lewis. I was talking
about Tolkien…back before the Greeks.
So, as I would've meant to say: I half
expected Gandalf to make a grand
appearance at any moment.

Winging It

October 13

I'm not sure what brought the odd
magic about, but part of it had to do
with the fact that my voice was shot to
hell. So, the song list would have to be
carefully chosen. I had one last show to
go, here at my friends' place in Florence,
before heading out to the airport in the
morning. But I knew that if I landed on
the perfect combination of Tylenol and
tequila, I should be able to pull this off.

I wanted to do something for the kids
murdered by hang gliders at the music
festival in Israel. But, some political or
war-protest song didn't feel right. Too
predictable. And the moment was still
too raw. And those kinds of songs require a tone of voice I couldn't carry.

Finally, it hit me: the story of the sweet
girl, and that song I sang her under my
breath—the one who'd brought me my
falafel sandwich there on the boardwalk

in Eilat, by the Red Sea? She came back
to me. And that's when I figured it out.
I should sing those kids a love song.
And, even better than that?…a Bob
Dylan love song. Because, who better
to cover when your voice is shot to hell,
than Bob Dylan?

So I told that story in the concert, and
explained my reasoning, then dedicated
"Make You Feel My Love" to those who
lost their lives for the sake of their love
for music. It caused a minor meltdown
among sensitive folks, stoic tears for a
few others, but a pin-drop silence in the
room overall. And so, everything (even
my vocal transgression) was forgiven,
for the rest of the performance.

Sometimes, you've gotta pivot. And
sometimes, it works, thank God. It
helped the rest of the evening go off
without a hitch—even if a bit off pitch.
To the point that it doesn't bother me at
all that I can't speak on the flight home.

Nor does it bug me that the gray-haired gentleman across the aisle sorted out his Southwest Snack Mix into separate like piles of nuts, pretzels, and little squares of Chex cereal. Nor did I get angry with the overly talkative dude in the middle seat who was obsessively-compulsively in love with the woman by the window, to the point I wanted to lean over and try to help him out by suggesting: *Buddy, you're killin' every chance you've got for this to last.*

Hell…I even did well not to worry about the fact that I was flying on Friday the 13th.

Mostly.

An Augury of Autumn

October 14

This afternoon, the pale ghost of the moon put on a black sheet and danced across the stage in front of the sun, turning it into an elven ring of fire— an event that humans long took to be serious, if not gravely so. At least until science convinced too many of us that stellar events are merely mathematically predictable recurrences. Therefore…to consider them signs, portents, or omens, is just silly.

But, if you're one of those, like me, who believes science is still in its infancy and, so, many hundreds of years behind in its research into astrological signs, portents, and omens, let's join hands and consider today's annular eclipse as a catalyst for radical and powerful transformation. A time of great change and forward movement. Heightened energy.

That softened light, filtering through the
leafy trees, cast crescent-like shadows on
the pavement like I've never seen in my
life. A kaleidoscopic display I desperately
do not want science to explain to me. I
need a little magic in my life. And so, a
greatly dimmed sun in the middle of a
cloudless day is just what the shaman
ordered.

The Doldrums

The storm is over; too bad, I say.
At least storms are clear
about their dangerous intent.

~ Stephen Dunn
"Ordinary Days"

When you feel a new life coming on,
there's a desire to leap in, and to get on
with it. You feel the urge to say: *Just tell
me where to go! And then, what to do when I
get there!* So, the normal days—the days
when you're not sitting at the feet of an
old Yaqui diablero learning about "the
dark sea of awareness," but, instead,
watching the Houston Texans play the
New Orleans Saints in football—can be
a bit troublesome.

Especially when you're watching with
your not-your-wife-anymore, because
you're still stuck in Texas, where it is, at
least, finally down to 68° outside, thank

God—or whoever's in charge. Because, it's been in the 80s and 90s, for heaven's sake.

The truth is, even Odysseus had to have off days. Sea travel by sail, back then, could not possibly have offered endless hours and weeks of excitement. (Ask any sailor.) Hell, he spent seven lost years on a luscious island under the constant care and loving attention of a beautiful, sexy goddess with sizzling dark braids, but still managed to be miserable anyway— eventually clawing his eyeballs out over boredom. Poor, gorgeous Calypso. She offered that weepy mortal everything— everything except the one thing that he wanted: a way home.

So, to deal with the doldrums, I think I'll head outside, stack some stones, build a fire, and let the stars remind me that home, The Sky, is an awfully big place.

And that even when I am here…
I am there.

Surviving Ogygia

October 17

The goal of Dissolution is
precisely to be torn apart, to be
dismembered so that we can be
subsequently reconfigured in a
never-before-seen pattern —

~ Bill Plotkin
The Journey of Soul Initiation

Wimberley, Texas now makes me feel
nervous. Locals might take it personally.
But it's no one's fault. The combination
of the place and its people just represent
the velvet rut that had sucked me down
and in to its grooves, where my needle
was endlessly skipping. What Plotkin
calls "everyday Village life."

There's nothing wrong with the town,
inherently. But it is anathema to my goal
for this year. It is my island of Ogygia…
where Calypso's trying to get me to stay.

It is the place where Carl Jung, in his *Red Book*, says:

> I was going about laden with
> thoughts of which I could speak
> to no one: they would only have
> been misunderstood. I felt the gulf
> between the external world and
> the interior world of images in its
> most painful form.

The problem is, I will have to drop my anchor in Wimberley between voyages. So…I need to keep a severe eye on it when I'm here. I need to recognize its sweet call back to normalcy. I've got to check myself against the swish and the swizzle of Calypso's enticing braids.

Because of my parents, my daughter, and finances, I will have to dance this delicate waltz while keeping a hard grip on the mission— the new mission I have to thoroughly lose myself—the controlling egocentric self that's been miserably wallowing in a vortex of victimhood, blind adherence, and dream-denial.

It doesn't mean I can't love what has been home for over a decade now. Nor does it mean I'll never return someday, in some way, to spend some amount of time. But, for this year, I must avoid at all costs what Plotkin says of Jung's Descent:

> If, on the other hand, he refuses the call and abandons the Descent, he could be assigning himself to a life of quiet desperation, preyed upon by a dominator culture — while at the same time being an agent of that very culture.

Back Out There

Soon enough, I'm back out sailing between those yellow and white lines again. The never-ending heartbreak of what I leave behind mingling with the unrelenting joy of a new freedom to wander the great maze of samsara—somewhere between lives, but always this side of nirvana.

I know the goal is the cessation of the cycle, the release from desire. The final liberation that leads to ultimate peace. But for now, I am just a Dharma Bum caught up in the love and the throes and the push-pull tides of the process. As Kerouac's Japhy Ryder says:

> I wanta swim in rivers and drink
> goatmilk and talk with priests and
> just read Chinese books and
> amble around the valleys talking
> to farmers and their children.

Yeah, me and Japhy all the way.

Parts of northwest Texas will crush the bones of your soul if you do not know how to be alone. When you're 53 miles from the nearest town, and all it offers when you get there is a Dollar General and a rundown Dairy Queen, you need to know who you are, down deep inside somewhere, when the sun sets. Or when it rises, for that matter. If you've got a desire of some kind, there aren't many ways to fulfill it out here. So it's best to be a Buddhist, if you can manage it.

The folks who live a mile over won't likely understand your meditatin' ways, though. So they'll be prayin' for your lost soul—you can bet—down at the Baptist church on Sunday. Which is nice—as it sort of doubles your chances at survival.

Parts of eastern New Mexico remind me how many "out theres" there are—out where nobody knows your name. And the yucca will not ask…nor will the diamondback care.

Out here, the yucca is known for its ability to survive on very little water, and on very little love. Just ask the coyote, or that cactus. They won't say anything. But the cackle of the one and needle prick of the other will give you the gist.

All of it together helps me not to forget there may come the time when I'm the only one who believes that what I'm doing makes any sense—and that my belief, alone, will need to be sufficient.

I'll need to cut every cord that binds me. Gnaw my own foot off if I have to. And I'll have to keep a good close watch on my mind as it shifts, like the sand out in this desert in the teeth of a hard wind.

Alone Again, Naturally

October 20

Sitting against a far wall in Iconik on Guadalupe in Santa Fe, I see that my whole life I've been in training for the kind of alone I am going to need to be this year. Going back to early childhood, being five and seven years younger than my two brothers made me feel like an only child. There was always a psychic distance between us. It still exists. But for different reasons now.

From kindergarten through 12th grade, I felt profoundly alone: in the halls, during class, or in the back of a bus. Pep rallies and school assemblies were tantamount to torture. Yet, they were no match for the purgatorial torment of girls. There is no alone like the aloneness of being an insanely shy male in the killing fields of middle and high school.

Ever since, I've been capable of being existentially alone in coffee shops, on packed flights, sitting in bars with people inches away on either side, and in line at banks and grocery stores. To be honest, I can be quite alone in the middle of my own performances.

An hour later, I'm comfortably alone at the five-stool bar in Maria's. I love bars. Bartenders are masters at leaving you alone. And, if you're in the right bar, they're also the masters of the second most important thing: making a proper margarita. (Yes, it's true, being left alone is actually more important.)

Even the scintillating young woman with seven piercings in her left ear sitting next to me—who seems intrigued, over bites of chicken taquitos, by my conviction to be alone—has no power to pull me out of it. No…I need a year to think. Or, a year to learn how to think less, and more often *just be* instead. (Which is big talk

coming from one who could possibly
succumb to the next set of earrings.)

I don't mean to sound grandiose. The
bottom line is as simple as it is necessary: I want to learn how to be alone
again—to find peace within solitude.

My house needs a better frame. And so,
a certain amount of tearing down has to
take place for that to be done properly.

A better person lives within me. I'll find
him. And he will have a lot to offer to a
hurting and confused world—having
been there and done both.

And you will learn in spite of
yourself; that's the rule.

~ Carlos Castaneda
The Teachings of Don Juan

Gone and Done

October 21

I drove over 900 miles to read poems and sing a few songs to nine people at the New Mexico State Poetry Society fundraiser in Albuquerque. All nine of them seemed to enjoy it. And every one of them sang along on the last verse of "We Shall Overcome" at the end. They paid me $100. And I sold $25-worth of product.

Afterwards, they apologized for the small size of the crowd. There was a lot of competition in town. I told them I *never* care about that. I had a great time. The main thing is that they keep doing the good and difficult work of poetry.

I packed my guitar, and the box still full of books-you-keep-wishing-would-sell, into the car and drove an hour back up to Santa Fe to hang out with my friend Paul White, while a couple of burgers and some mashed potatoes cooked.

And I'm not sure I will ever be able to
craft a reasonable explanation (writer
that I'm supposed to be) for why I
would do such a thing. But, it has
something to do with what the truck
driver, Beaudry, says to Ray in *The
Dharma Bums*:

> Here I am killin myself drivin this
> rig back and forth from Ohio to
> L.A. and I make more money than
> you ever had in your whole life as
> a hobo, but you're the one who
> enjoys life and not only that but
> you do it without workin or a
> whole lot of money. Now who's
> smart, you or me?

Though I prefer vagabond to hobo,
there is something of the deathbed
confession in his words. Something
about going ahead and doing now
what I would have otherwise said—
in my last breath—that I wish I had
gone and done, long before it was
too late.

9+9 = Infinity

October 22

I have it from a firsthand account that last night—just a few hours after I had performed for nine people in a senior center in Albuquerque—that back in my not-my-town-anymore, Paul Simon had showed up at a Saturday night shindig at the photography gallery of a friend down near the square.

Paul—and yes, that's as in Simon and Garfunkel—though Paul might not appreciate me saying that—is now a resident of Wimberley, Texas.

Anyway, the friend had live music going on the front porch of his gallery. And, as the evening slipped on toward darkness, Paul stepped over to the musician after a song (who was more than willing to yield his guitar—best night of *his* life) to ask if he could play a tune. And the master sat down and played "Slip Slidin' Away" to—are you ready for it?—yes, an

audience of nine people standing, utterly
dumbfounded, in the parking lot, with
traffic buzzing by on Farm to Market
Road 12.

I cannot tell you the register of seismic
waves this sent up and down my spine.
The sheer cosmic balance of it all. The
camaraderie. The vindication.

Those eighteen people, between us, who
were served up our best…and our long-
suffering as artists.

The beauty of it. The brotherhood.

Thank you, Sir Paul, for showing us—
through such a simple action—what it
all comes down to.

The Thin Places

October 23

The early Dawn was born;
    her fingers bloomed.

The Odyssey – Book 2:1

Dawn plays a major character in *The Odyssey*. She shows up often and usually has something to do with blooming or "rosy fingers." She always introduces some new scene in the play. She wakes us up to change—the next morning's raising of the sails.

Dawn is one of life's great liminal spaces—one of those "in between" places. As is dusk. Two highly spiritual times of a day that I need to take more seriously. The type of silence they ride in and out on is so different from the other hours of any day—silence being another liminal space I crave. So a quiet dawn or a quiet dusk doubles down on liminality.

And I should greet them with more
reverence, and more often, than I do.

I went to great effort to make sure I
witnessed, and was deeply present for,
the rising of the rosy sun on the new
millennium 23 years ago. I sat on top
of a 20-foot berm at the western edge
of the Westwood Golf Course in my
hometown and watched it "break out"
on the eastern horizon. I cried. Nothing
unusual for me. I can burst into tears
from watching a kitten yawn, or hearing
the opening notes of Snow Patrol's song
"Chasing Cars." That guitar riff lives at
the heart of a hundred memories for me.

But encountering the soul of that particular sunrise gave me a deep blessing.
Or, I want to say: a power—one I still
carry with me. Like a secret talisman I
keep in my invisible bag of spiritual
tools.

And it helps preserve the dear memory
of the night before, when I'd stood in
my first ex-wife's kitchen—while she

was curled up on the couch with a new boyfriend—and slow danced with my three-and-a-half-year-old daughter sound asleep and slobbering on my shoulder, as the big Times Square ball dropped and counted down to the first second of the next set of one thousand years. A profoundly liminal instant I had carefully orchestrated, at great pains and sacrifice—as well as to the quite notable consternation…but eventual acquiescence…of my ex.

Sierra may not remember the moment herself. But she can know, now, that it happened—and what it looked like.

So it is that I write this morning for the black-ink reminder that I need to keep moving, more and more, towards the "thin places," as the Irish call them. Those ethereal spaces made more of energy than matter—where we walk between this world and some other that offers transformation.

Sunrise on 66

I beat the sun getting up this morning
and was on I-25 North with nothing
but a thin gray strip of barely-light on
the eastern horizon ahead of me. Later,
as I crossed over the Pecos River, sparse
clouds turned into bright pink heralds of
the sun's yawning approach on its way
to work. But when I got to the big curve
at Bernal, it broke out in a blaze over the
shoulder of Starvation Peak. From there
on, it danced with the mesas—ducking
behind, then popping back out again—
most of the way down 84 to Santa Rosa.

By the time I made Tucumcari, the rays
of our home-star were warming up I-40
and making it hard to see heading east.
And so, as the Doobie Brothers were
jammin' on the car stereo with "Long
Train Running," I decided to stop in at
Kix on 66 for the Rise & Shine breakfast
special:

Scrambled Eggs, Hash Browns,
Sourdough Toast, and
"Corn Beef Hash."

The place started out as a Denny's back
in the 1950s. And though Kix is a new-
ish iteration, the dark-green Naugahyde
barstools and booths feel of a century.
About as old as the coffee tastes, and
about as old as the Roadrunner Lodge
across Route 66 looks to be. Where the
marquis below the sign reads:

GIVE THE
INTERSTATE
THE BIRD

Both the corned beef and the browns
were very hashy, but very tasty. And the
sourdough toast was as thick as a classic
novel. But when Joe Cocker came on the
ceiling speakers croak-singing "You Are
So Beautiful," I had to leave before he
cracked on those last two words. Too
heartbreaking for me right now.

The bill was $9.72. So, I left two fives and three ones from the sale of the book and two CDs in Albuquerque, thanked my sweet, loquacious waitress, and then headed for the door right before Joe choked on "to…me…"

From one end to the other of Route 66 through Tucumcari, the roadsides are littered with the shipwrecks and burned out hulls of old abandoned hotels, gas stations, and curio shops—just like the remnants of Odysseus's failures, filled with the ghosts of his poor sailors who did not make it home.

So, it didn't really matter whether I escaped the end of Joe's song or not.

One way or another, heartbreak's gonna catch up with you—somewhere, some-how—along this lonesome highway.

Hard to Tell

October 25

Highway 152 in western Oklahoma is a good way to avoid I-40. It drops down a nice safe distance from that Devil Road, 66. And it runs, much more straight and narrow, through a very rural territory occupied by solid, conservative folks, who aren't long on irony. All my dad's people came from this land, and stock.

Somewhere on the give or take side of Binger (a town my dad played against in baseball), a standard, Department-of-Transportation-looking road sign—the thermoplastic green with white letters—reads:

At least that's what I think it said. It was
riddled with bullet holes. So it was hard
to make out some of the words.

Such a bizarre act of conservative-on-
conservative violence playing out in that
frame. It's sort of a symbol of the utter
disarray of the Republican Party these
days.

I appreciated, though, the way those
bullet holes served as punctuation. It
drives the professor in me crazy when
they leave off the commas and question
marks on signs like that.

Love and Deoxyribonucleic Acid

October 27

On the final stretch of the long drive last night, I got the call from Mom that they were in a minor emergency clinic waiting on the ambulance to take Dad over to Methodist Hospital in San Antonio for an appendectomy. So, I knew now there would be no rest for my weariness when I got back. The next few days, or more, would be full of white tiles, elevators, scrubs, and stale coffee in Styrofoam.

I was up in the morning and off to their assisted living cottage down in Boerne— one of those sad suburbs created out of the colonization and commodification of what used to be a cute little town. Mom needed me to gather up a few necessities for them.

Being in their new quarters without them there, filled me with a gripping melancholy that made me want to rush through the task. The emptiness of that

space made me flinch from a dark sense
of foreshadowing that I didn't want to
sit with. So I got right to it.

Gathering up your dad's clothes and
underclothes is a soft reminder of the
million and one things your parents have
done for you over a lifetime—the self-
sacrifice that blossoms out of a form of
love that can only be understood by a
parent.

Yet even as parents, we never fully grasp
the nature and power of what it is we do
without thinking about it—at least most
of the time. The survival of any species
rides on DNA triggers as much as love.

And so it is that my love and DNA will
guide me through this day…

    or week…

    or more.

Depression Personified

October 30

It's always a little more likely in Texas.
But, it can strike anywhere, anytime.

And I say strike, but it's really more like
a patient assassin who's in no hurry to
kill you, because he enjoys the process.
He loves to listen to Pavarotti sing that
sad Puccini song from *Turandot* on the
playlist he made for work nights. (And I
can't believe I am just now noticing the
word "assassin" has two "asses" in it.)

And I don't know why I would portray
depression as a "he." For me, she's really
more of a "she." One of those sultry and
sexy shes you secretly want to go to bed
with, but you know she's more trouble
than she's worth. You've been down
that road of ramifications before.

But still, you're wishy-washy about it
anyway. And so, you linger over your
thoughts. Which gives her enough time

to slip up behind you—patient assassin
that she is—and wrap her arms around
your front, with her right hand firmly on
what counts.

Now she's got you. And you think: *Well,
how bad could one night be? Really.* But you
know how that dark song ends. Yes…
that hard needle points due north. Until
the whole thing goes south…and then
the portly lady sings.

The lights dim. The curtain falls. And by
the middle of the night, there are socks,
a bra, and empty shot glasses strewn all
about the place. And you can already
feel the headache coming on.

Sweet Death

October 31

Here on the hallowed eve of All Saints Day, I am sitting in a favorite spot at Poetic Republic on South Presa in San Antonio thinking about how scary life and death can be. And, this year, more than ever.

One of the things I love about this holiday is the way it makes ghosts and witches…spiders and their webs…seem normal. Cute even. And how blood and tombstones…skulls and their bones… serve as innocent reminders of the hard truths about life, and where the whole thing is ultimately headed.

And tomorrow—Day of the Dead, Dia de Los Muertos, All Saints, or whatever you want to call it—marks the annual moment when the dead are said to cross back over the threshold, walk among us, and remind us of those same things in their own ways.

Hospitals do much the same. But they're not as fun as Halloween. They're sterile, and you don't get any candy when you knock on doors. But they do serve their purpose—as Methodist is doing for Dad right now.

And that's where I will head when I'm done here at the coffee shop, where the two baristas are costumed up as Cheech and Chong—and where my Gingerbread Man cookie was covered in red stitches, had black buttons and eyes, and a black bandage over his brown forehead, with a sprinkling of orange glitter all over him.

Pobrecito. Poor little guy. I'll have to finish off what's left of him.

Yes, this morning I ate Sweet Death for breakfast. I showed no mercy. And why should I? He'd have none for me.

~ November ~

A Big Day

November 1

Often, it is when the artist and the
poet seem least occupied with
their work that they are most
profoundly absorbed in it.

~ Pierre Larousse

Allhallowtide, or the Hallowmas season,
when we remember the saints and souls
who have gone before us, is a time of
liminality—when the line between the
living and the dead is very thin. Some
believe there's a bit of crossing back and
forth going on. And I'm fine either way.
Though I'm more convinced than ever
that most of the lines we try to draw can
get pretty damn thin now and then.

So, just before dawn, here on All Saints Day, I bundled up—because it's actually chilly in Texas—and went outside to greet the sunrise over a stand of gray oaks off in the distance.

In a back corner of the property, I came upon a large flat stone I am shocked I hadn't yet noticed for its nobleness, as well as location. It's just thick enough to make a good low seat, and it lays in a perfect spot to view the sun's gentle appearance.

I cleared some weeds and rocks to make a space for my feet. And that's when I spotted an old rotting corner fence post wrapped in a tangle of rusted barbed wire from another age. Just one more line someone tried to draw that was doomed to fail. Behind that stands a strikingly smooth gray skeleton tree about fifteen feet tall—a perfect decoration for Halloween.

When I turned back to the east, some soft rays of first light were bouncing off

the big picture windows of a house high
on top of the hill to the south. There
was no sign of the bright burning disc
itself yet, down where I was sitting,
but it was imminent.

That's when I began to pray to the Great
Spirit. Which, I must say, is quite a new
thing for me.

I invoked healing, for my dad. Peace and
stamina, for my mom. And I asked for
strength and courage for dear friends,
Tommy and Betty, who got some very
scary news yesterday, on Halloween.

I begged to be filled with and consumed
by kindness—as a way of being. And as
the tip of the sun broke through the
trees, I proclaimed that it's time to
dissolve the business of my previous
life—to enter the cocoon—and then
wait…in the hope for a new pair of
wings. Because, it is never too late—
even for a fuzzy old caterpillar like me.

At the tail-end of this unusual bout of
intercession, a striking red-cockaded
woodpecker landed on the skeleton tree
with a sharp squeak-chirp, then he went
straight to his rat-tat-tatting. A bit of tiny
magnificence. He didn't care at all about
my presence and stayed at his work.
Tap-tap…rat-tat-tat.

And by this point in my journey, no one
has to tell me about the soul-significance
of these feathered creatures. How they
symbolize freedom—the bond-breaking
of weight and gravity. They signify living
on thresholds—at home on Earth, and
in The Sky.

They are the omen of all omens—the
totem of totems. And so, I accepted the
blessing, the reward for my early rising,
and thanked the good saints and souls
who came before me and smiled down
on my prayer.

A Bigger Day

All Souls Day is a bigger event for me now. Bigger in the sense that I am inviting in a wildly higher number of souls this time—and from here on.

I've not cleared it with the Vatican. But I doubt Pope Francis will worry too much about the declarations of a discontinued Southern Baptist preacher's kid. Besides, I believe his namesake would agree with me all the way to the woods and back. Because I'm bringing in All Souls—the souls of the birds, the souls of the bees, the souls of all the animals and trees, the souls of all mountains and seas. Not just the human souls missing their bones, but also the souls of the rocks and stones.

If it's not some plastic-synthetic-petro-chemical-based abomination of man, then that soul, my friends, is in.

The In-betweens

Back at Common Grounds up in Waco, I'm listening to two coeds on the couch next to my table talk not quite to each other—as they fondle their phones— about what their suburban futures will look like. There is a good amount of confidence in their well-thought-out materialistic plans. The volume of the voices alone works like an exclamation point at the end of all their ontological certainties. And, I think I just heard a finger snap.

Fortunately, the me I am changing into no longer feels tempted to lean over and say: *Oh, good luck, ladies—sounds absolutely dreadful.* Because I see now the part that the college years play in our lives. How creating a God in the image of our wants and needs can serve as a survival mech- anism in the madness of suspended adolescence.

I compare it to my complete loss of all
certainty—about anything. I no longer
know what home means—especially
whenever I'm where I thought it was
going to be. And, I don't know where
I'm going either, whenever I leave there.
Which is a lot. I just arrive in places, for
a little while, then move on to the next
wherever.

That may be why I'm most comfortable
when I'm in between those places. Like
here, in this coffee shop on the edge of
Baylor University, listening to all of the
youthful religious conviction around me.

Like these two guys at the table on the
other side of that couch, talking about
girls, God, and Corvettes. It's easier to
flex the wings of the new me in spaces
where no one knows the old one. But
also when I'm in the car, sailing on the
roads of America, where God and I can
be ourselves together…   silent…
and free of all expectations.

Keeping the Fire

November 4

The road brought me this time up to Oklahoma City to read a few poems for the Lighting of the Fires ceremony at Full Circle Bookstore. They've done it for many years, and I have participated several times, because the place has been so good to me, actively recommending and selling my books.

Jim Tolbert is an Oklahoma icon who, among other accomplishments, made sure this city was going to have a world-class independent bookstore—one with wood floors and rolling ladders, a lovely little café, three fireplaces, and a poetry section to beat most other stores that have mostly given up on it as a genre. He's the owner and had requested my presence at the event. So, this is one of those non-paying gigs you drive twelve hours roundtrip to do.

At five minutes to noon, four people had gathered around the first fireplace where we would begin. Bill Merickel—a retired news cameraman, and my partner in performance—pulled out his wooden flutes, some dark sage in a half sea shell, and a bundle of turkey feathers for the smudging ceremony. And by five after, when Jim was about to open up with his story of the fireplaces and why they were so important to him, there were, all of a sudden, 30 to 40 people leaning against bookshelves or standing on tiptoes back by the registers.

Jim spoke, I read a poem about fire and stone, then Bill lit the sage, swirled the smoke with the feathers, and finished with a brief flute piece. The fire was sparked. It popped into flame. And, after a bit of gazing, we moved to the next fireplace to do the same.

I know it may seem like little to nothing, here on the silent page. But sometimes moments add up to more than the sum of the characters playing their parts.

By the end, more than 50 of us had gathered in this beautiful sanctuary of literature and art to honor the written word and the fire that burns to keep the hope for enlightenment alive—both the physical fire to light our reading, and the spiritual fire that glows in those who still believe in its absolute necessity to the survival of civilization.

And so it is that I will follow the trail of this spirit for as long as my body is able.

What I Didn't Know Then

November 5

In my hometown, I stand in the dirt circle of homebase in the old ballfield out in a back corner of my elementary schoolyard. And I recall how miserable I felt trying to achieve competence in the normal boy activities of those early grades—as well as all the grades that followed.

I had a healthy fear of failure back then. Mainly because I failed at most of those masculine mile markers. And I didn't know yet it was possible to excel at the other things I was good at, and still be considered a man. The chief problem being, I didn't yet know they existed.

So, for me, in the fourth or fifth grade, there was a lot of "swing-and-a-miss," along with flubbing the grounder out in left field. And I don't know the extent to which those days still mess with these days in my life. But I probably shouldn't overanalyze it.

And yet, when it comes to marriage, I've just swung and missed for the second time. *Strike two!* I hear the little demon on my right shoulder say. And out beyond that, I hear the catcalls of long-ago teammates jeering me onto a third.

It's a much more cruel age, at least for some kids, than parents want to believe. I wouldn't go back. Just like, in five to ten years, I won't wanna come back to now.

So, here in the shadows of this Fallen Autumn, I should continue to excel at the things I'm good at. Because now, I have learned that all the swings-and-misses, and all the catcalls and jeers that follow, don't matter. I know now what I was ordained by destiny to do. And I'm doing it well…dammit.

Minding My Own Consciousness

November 6

Toward the end of a tough conversation with Ashley last night, that finished a bit strained, I received a great and terrible gift. My consciousness shifted outside my body, just in front of me, where I could see my face—the troubles, pain, and subsequent fear of damage done to me long before this relationship. It killed me to see what she was seeing—and long has been.

The "great" part of the gift is that I got a hard and clear picture—a cold vision— of the old part of me that was going to (no other way to put it) have to die, if I'm ever going to live into a better and truer version of myself. For some tough reason, I needed to *see* it—in order to know how to target it.

The "terrible" part of it comes in the emerging understanding of what it's going to take to kill that part of me.

It will be a death—an absolute parting
with something I believed was critical
and defensible for a half of my lifetime.
A sad badge I thought I was supposed to
wear.

Then, during the night, came two more
visions—in the form of dreams. One,
very brief, had Ashley holding the rope
and harness on a beautiful brown horse.
She handed me the rope, and it began to
slip out of the harness. The horse bit the
rope and pulled once or twice, but then
stepped back and ran off. Basically, I'd
dreamed of an analogy about trust that
Ashley had given me over a year ago in a
letter she'd written me.

The second dream was an extraordinary
scene of an expansive blue sky that had a
huge and powerful river gushing out of a
giant seam in it that created a roaring
waterfall into nothingness.

I'm not much on interpretation. I think
assigning meaning hinders the work of
dreams. But, as a Pisces whose home is

now The Sky, that second one is rife. So it's hard not to go all Freudian and Jungian on it.

All I know right now is that I perceive them as significant. Dreams so seldom linger with me. I hardly ever remember them after a day, if I can recall them at all. Though, that seems to be changing of late. So let's just hold onto those for down the vagabond road.

Button Up

November 7

I had low expectations. But a friend in
New Mexico had given me two small
dried buttons of peyote—a very rare
offering that should not be wasted.
He said it wasn't enough to do much.
Just enough to give a taste of what it's
like—a taste he warned me would be
"yucky," to use his technical term.
(Probably why humans are one of
its only predators.)

So, I had fasted from the night before,
and in the late afternoon, I put a cup of
water on to boil. I dropped the hard gray
buttons in—having no idea how long
they're supposed to steep. He'd said to
boil them until they got soft. But, from
the original texture, I doubted that they
would reach any point beyond "kind of
gushy"—to use my technical term.

After 20 minutes, I turned off the heat,
let them sit a bit, then forked them out,

and poured the tea into a mug hand-
made by my friend, Lynde, in Oregon.

It went down easily, and didn't taste all
that bad, really. From there, I put on my
work pants and boots, because the next
point of instruction was to place the two
mushy buttons under my tongue for two
hours. I wasn't certain this was protocol.
He might've just been messing with me.
But my sweet daughter (who, mind you,
has never done anything wrong—and,
therefore, knows nothing about these
things) told me I *must* follow my guide's
advice.

The plan was to build a fire and stack
rocks for the two hours, while I waited
for some kind of sensation to kick in…
which it never did…which frustrated me
and made me feel like I must've done it
wrong somehow. But I powered on, and
when time was up, I chewed those yucky
suckers to a pulp and swallowed.

Turns out my friend had been right on
one point at least: the taste. Something

along the lines of shoe leather meets a
tree root with the dirt still clinging to it.

I'm embarrassed by my impatience. But
that's what I was feeling by this point.
So, within minutes, I went up and made
a margarita and cooked a small supper of
a jalapeño turkey burger patty on top of
asparagus, onion, and poblano. I took it
all back down to the fire and sipped and
ate very slowly, right down to the last bit
of vermillion light in the western sky.

Soon, the fire was the only natural light.
And that happened to be the time I first
thought, *Hmm…wait a minute.* I felt an
extraordinary mellowness begin to creep
in. I oozed down in my chair, gazed into
the oracular flames, and wondered
where this was going.

I wouldn't call it high, or wasted. It felt
more like something just this side of it.
But it certainly qualified as an alteration.
And it reiterates the total inadequacy of
words when it comes to things like this.

At the peak, I had an overwhelming, and I mean profound, sensation of okayness.

It's okay. You're okay. None of it matters. Forgive. Forgive your fears. Forgive others theirs. There is nothing wrong with you. The coming changes in you are all right on time. It all had to happen…all 58 years of it…in order to bring you where you had to be. There was no way around it. Now you must wait here, inside the cocoon. Transformation takes time. But there are wings on the other side of this.

Oh, how I wanted to stay there in that kaleidoscopic cloud. I wanted to build a home in the mist of that peace But, alas, these adventures don't work that way.

I can tell you this, though: I will likely come back again…given half a chance, and a couple more buttons.

Split Open

November 8

Feeling more okay with things doesn't keep me from contemplating the heavy mysteries of loss and love. It just helps me to see them more for what they are. Like the news from an old friend that the first love of my life, Pamela Durso, died of a stroke a few days ago.

Pam was the self-appointed queen of our neighborhood kid-gang days on the streets of Westwood Estates. And I was most often her king. (One would never have been enough for her.)

If we played House, she took Mom, I took Dad. Cops and Robbers? I was the Cop, she the Robber—for reasons you'll see. Cowboys and Indians? (And, I am sorry, but that is what we called it, and that is what we played.) I would be the Cowboy, and she would channel the Native Princess.

Though we were the same age, Pam was
born into the psyche of a 25-year-old.
So, by the time we were rubbing up
against each other on the threshold of
our early teens, she was somewhere in
the late 30s of her soul. And that soul
was dark and sultry. She seethed with
sexual savviness before I understood
that a body could wear that like sweet
perfume. She knew of carnal things I
was desperate to figure out.

For our very first kiss, she dragged me
around the side of some house, pulled
me in, and split open my pubescent
world with her tongue. None of that
messin' around with limp wet lips.

And though we never made love, there
came that one humid summer night in
the warm grass beside the garage of my
house where that sad fallen angel pretty
much explained—without words—how
it worked…well enough that this little
preacher's boy was sure he was goin'
straight to Hell.

Pam was the beautiful mistake—the one
parents hoped you would not make—
that blesses the young days of shy and
sensitive boys who are lucky enough to
survive the mentorship.

And I, for one, am grateful. As grateful
as I am we did not end up together.

Though, in the wake of the surprising
and sorrowful news of her death, I find
myself missing her…terribly.

Hanging in the Gallery

November 9

I'm just a little down tonight
I'm just a little down
just a little messed up is all I'm sayin'

~ James McMurtry, "Restless"

At times, it's better to receive than give.
So I drive into Austin on a Wednesday,
wander up South Congress Avenue, grab
a big piece of pepperoni pizza at Home
Slice, eat it on the curb, then walk back
down to the fire escape stairs that lead
up to the back door of the Gallery above
the Continental Club, where James lets
me in after a hard secret knock.

It's 30 minutes before they'll open the
doors for the line around the side of the
building. His solo show, every week he's
in town, is very popular. And while he
tunes his 12-string (because they require
as much attention as any fussy princess),
I talk to Kellie behind the bar while she

preps the bottles and glasses and cuts
limes into perfect wedges.

She tells me too many people they know
have died lately. That…or they're in the
process. Or they're in a hospital trying
not to. And I say a *Yes* to that last one.

When the lights dim, the Gallery glows
dark neon red. When James straps on his
guitar, the smart people shut up. And,
any dumb ones, the smart ones turn to
shut them up. We're here for the words:

> *I ain't got a place*
> *I ain't got a place in this world I know*

Whatever message I need, McMurtry's
likely to have it. His case of "Been there,
done that," is more severe than most.

> *You got to me*
> *Brought all this empty down on top of me*
> *I didn't know, but we were not to be*
> *But I know a thing or two now*

I huddle up in the window sill by the bar
where Kellie slips me a salty Kellierita—
a margarita made with more skill and
love than most tenders have. BettySoo,
over at her stool, eyes closed, sings along
to his heart-bending song "Cutter," as
she wipes years from her eyes.

> *So I can keep it down out of sight*
> *Way off to the side*
> *It won't come at me on a dark cold night*
> *The red ridges I can't hide…*
> *they're on the outside*

James has a lot of fans. But he also has
disciples—a higher tier. It's those who
know all the words to his songs. And
there's a small choir of them at the tiny
bar back in the shadows who harmonize
every Wednesday night. Angels on black
velvet—each an artist in her own right.

So, at the end of the show, I like to go
over and mingle with the dark angels—
get as close as I can to what I'm not sure
I understand.

A Little Sensitive Maybe?

November 12

geography *n.* 1 The branch of knowledge that deals with the earth's surface, its form and physical features, natural and political divisions, climate, products, population, etc.

geology *n.* 2 The branch of science that deals with the physical structure and substance of the earth, the processes which act on these, and the earth's development since its formation.

~ Oxford English Dictionary

The distinction between the two may seem subtle to some. But it's not. One deals with surface features, the other with what's going on down below us. Stones and trees exist, naturally, in both realms. For example, the shepherd's tree, of the Kalahari Desert, sinks its roots

down over 200 feet. So, tell me again
who's boss of the world?

It is a well-known fact, at least to me,
that I am highly sensitive to all things
geographical and geological. Well…at
least my rock and stone problem is fairly
well documented. But I also happen to
be a great lover—a regular Casanova—
of trees. One of many things I write too
often about is how, as a kid, *all* I wanted
to be when I grew up was Tarzan. I'd
call it an obsession. So I *lived* in the elm
trees of my elementary schoolyard and
the golf course near our house. I would
lie in their branches for hours. I *actually*
hugged them. Still do.

Yes, that love never died. I still converse
with trees. Usually when I'm alone. But
I'll break it out in front of other people,
if I feel so moved. I do not use a high-
pitched voice, like dog or cat people; I'll
speak in soft low tones, if not a whisper.
It's the same with the stones.

But places—both geographically and
geologically—will speak to me as well.
Words aren't necessary. I'd call it more
of a knowing. Like that close friend you
only need eye contact with when you're
in a room full of idiots together. I *feel*
when I'm in good places. And I *know*
when one is bad. I'll turn around and
walk away without explanation. And
while I've had encounters with both
extremes, most places exist somewhere
on the energetic spectrum in between.

On the extremes, the time I stood on a
razor peak high above Manoa Falls on
the island of Oahu, and could see the
Pacific Ocean in all four directions, was
a moment I shared with Earth that I will
never get over—a zenith of no-going-
back to a life of blithe indifference to
this planet and its dying wishes. I burst
into tears, gushed with emotion. My
body vibrated with waves of a beautiful,
ethereal energy—a spiritual force. I was
only *barely* able to peel myself away from
that holy spot and start back down the
mountain before it became too dark to

see. But along the way, while I still had
some daylight, I witnessed a full-circle
rainbow between me and the deep valley
below. A celestial blessing to send me on
my way.

On the darker end, returning home from
Nashville sometime in my 20s, I took a
state highway parallel and to the north of
I-40. One that I didn't know would dead
end at the Mississippi River. The closer I
got to the liquid state line, the deeper the
bar ditches got. I also noticed the houses
were on stilts. And, as I went, the stilts
got taller, and the truck tires got bigger.

All I know to say is that, at a certain
point, an invisible, yet somehow dark
and ominous, cloud descended on me.
A force—and I'll go ahead and say: Evil.
I was in the wrong place. And it was the
wrong time. The wrong century, even.

So, when I finally came to a low stretch
where the water was up over the road,
and it got near to the car frame on the
front wheels, I'd had enough of omens.

I backed up clear of it, turned around, and hightailed it out of the valley of the shadow of death. And, I actually *felt* it when I drove out of that cloud. There was a sea change in the quality of the ether around me.

Whether anyone else believes me, this subtle superpower informs many of the stories and poems I write. And so, it seems like critical information.

The Clash

That last chapter now brings me to the geo-sensitive issue of Texas—the state of my birth. And, currently, the state of the greatest glitch in my life, so far. To quote the British punk band, The Clash, and that madly indecisive song of theirs: *Should I stay or should I go?* Yes, that is the question. And the quandary it imposes is Shakespearean.

I must leave this house. So I no longer call it home. The Austin-San Antonio suburban complex—a sort of housing projects for the upper-middle-class—is stupidly expensive to live in, and even ridiculous, considering the waterless desert it's slated to be, sooner or later, because of the huge number of coastals flocking here, combined with a notably disgruntled planet making the summers an oven for the gods to bake their loaves of ambrosia in.

The little town of Wimberley, where this house is, sits between those two swelling conurbations and will be swallowed up by them before the water's gone. So my geographical sensors are metering in the red. They clearly say: *Time to go, buddy.*

Now for the rub. For one, my body's primal bio-ingredients were mixed and combined from the hard elements of this ruggedly individual land. I am a living byproduct of its dust and ashes. Next up, my parents will now pass their final years in a suburb of San Antonio, with no hope for parole. Thirdly, my daughter moved from Oklahoma to Austin just to be closer to us. And then, I also have five furry beings at this house I have come to love quite dearly.

And what I save for the last, is far from the least. The stones. Both the old Fire Pit, on a lot next to our previous place closer to town, and the Fire Circle here have been the headquarters for my soul for years. They are thin places…safe spaces. They hold me. I trust them…

126

can grieve among them. They assuage my fears and anger. Because there, by the sacred flames, under a holy moon surrounded by a choir of stars, I know who I am—and that who I am becoming will be even better.

Therefore, some of my geological and geographical sensors keep reading: *Stay*.

Great.

Now I'm thinking about the rest of the chorus in that Clash song:

> *If I go, there will be trouble.*
> *And if I stay, it will be double.*

Which only makes the absurd-to-begin-with situation even worse.

This Side of Nirvana

November 16

Near the end of Kerouac's *The Dharma Bums*, Ray is picked up on his hitchhike to Desolation Peak by a guy he describes as "a sweet young mustached one-kidney Bodhisattva Okie."

And it strikes me: Now there's a term I could add to "vagabond." Man, I could own Bodhisattva Okie: a native son of Oklahoma who is able to reach nirvana, but delays doing so out of compassion in order to save suffering beings.

Where do I sign?

I mean, I may have to change the subtitle of these books to:

The Birth of a Bodhisattva Okie.

Golden Arches
and Big Purple Bells

November 17

Now comes the sadness of
coming back to cities …

~ Ray Smith
The Dharma Bums

Kerouac ends his bummy little novel on Desolation Peak in the northern reaches of Washington State, near the border of Canada. It's Ray's very last day as a fire-spotter for the forest service. The lonely summer ends, and so they call all of the spotters down from their mountain tops.

In his first week, Ray had thought that he might die before his 60 days was up. The weather—the wind and cold—was maniacal, yet mixed in with clear, calm days of insane, indescribable beauty. But he tried to describe it anyway. And now, as he packs up to leave, he is seized with

a sadness over what he will return to:
people who've not seen the moon in
years, because they never turn their
televisions off.

This morning, I was seized by the same
as I drove down into San Antonio from
the northwest on I-10. Concrete, steel,
road construction, and the sick debris it
leaves. Six lanes per side and unbroken
chains of taillights. And a never-ending
rubber stamp of signage and big-box
corporate eyesores: iridescent-stained
oil-change caves; the doleful fronts of
sub sandwich franchises; the darkness
behind every Walmart "Neighborhood
Market" raining down from Arkansas;
the fading golden arches; and the big
purple bells on top of taco joints. And
one rectangle monstrosity just called
itself The Rug Store.

The eternal stretch and stench of it is
wretched and profoundly depressing—
these malignant tumors of the American
Dream…the zenith of unoriginality…a
monocultural death knell of civilization.

One dystopian vision of the near future predicts that parts of certain interstates will become seamless cities that cross multiple state borders. One example being I-35. So, imagine Kansas City, Oklahoma City, Dallas/Fort Worth, Austin, and San Antonio as a single urban unit with no breaks or spaces between the rubber stamps of those corporate chains. That's 827 miles of solid sprawl, visible from outer space.

And this is our improvement on the natural order of the 4.5 billion years or so that preceded our species? So this is our geographical masterpiece—well-lit asphalt scars, endlessly lined with a pox of glowing concrete megastores?

I'll leave the answers to those questions to the historians and extraterrestrials… while I stick a thumb out and hitchhike my way back to Desolation Peak.

After 33 Years

November 18

We met in Jerusalem in our early to mid 20s. She spoke several languages, piloted small planes, and was well on her way to a Ph.D. at Hebrew University. I spoke rudimentary English, was terrified of small aircraft, and had no idea I would someday earn a Ph.D. as well—after 24 years of higher education.

She and her now husband flew into San Antonio from Montreal yesterday for him to do a presentation at an academic conference. So we made a plan to meet for lunch today. And I drove over from Dad's therapy facility to their hotel on the River Walk—a bit nervous about seeing her again.

The shy reunion out in front of the Westin—where they force you to let them park your car, for $25 (which is several meals for me on the road)— turned out to be sweet and relaxed, and rather unceremonial. It was great to see her again, and very nice to meet him. Conversation breezed along.

I'd made the questionable choice that we would walk down the river—which, let's be honest, is more of a multi-channeled cesspool—to a San Antonio classic for the meal. Mi Tierra. The Mi Tierra that opened with three tables in 1941, tables placed there by Pedro and Cruz Cortez. Mi Tierra, which now seats over 500. Mi Tierra, the Disneyland of Tex-Mex that looks like the aftermath of an exploded piñata the size of an Abrams M1 combat tank. Mi Tierra, where you can feel the heartbreak, and the spit, of the Mariachi band leaning over your table so far, a guitar string almost clips your ear.

And I need to stop with that. This story is about Michele and Daniel. But, also, about two people who had been in love over 35 years ago—a young love that was doomed by the 7,000 miles that separated us after I had to leave Israel.

This is about it never being too late to say hello again, and to reacquaint over margaritas and chile rellenos. And it's a bit about me wondering what happens to love, and whether it will come again to me—even whether or not I would want it to.

Anyway, I think everyone had a good time. I did. We traded hugs and got the valet to snap a shot of us after he pulled the car up. And I drove away, while my dad—I found out later that night—had taken my mom's hand, from his hospital bed, looked intently into her eyes, after 70 years, and said: *No matter what happens here…You…have been the love of my life.*

System Failure

November 19

I opened my laptop this morning to yet another sermon, in this year of sermons, on the nature and guarantee of inevitable impermanence—a black screen with just a white exclamation point inside a white circle telling me that all is lost—at least where my data is concerned.

And I thought: *You know? in comparison to so many other people on this planet, I have so little data. And all I ask is that that small portion be kept safe.*

Alas, hard drives, like life and marriage, sometimes fail. And so we have to start from scratch.

As one technically-inclined friend told me: *Well, your computer tried to start, but couldn't, and then tried recovery mode, but…*

And I didn't reply: *Well, I hardly see how that helps me.*

Besides, I've been working on restarting
and recovery for a long time now, and
my brain is still a blank screen.

So, there's no use sitting here and staring
at it. I just need to pull myself up and my
shoulders back, and do what any other
Bodhisattva Okie would do after an F-4
tornado: sift through the devastation…
and then begin to rebuild.

Best Seat in the House

November 21

A low-lying hedge of clouds held the sun at bay behind their curtain for a while— the orchestra still tuning. But it insisted upon rising and turning on the lights for the day. Another thread of clouds at the bottom, riding on the farthest horizon, suddenly burst into incandescence, as they drifted imperceptibly to the north. A wider stream of purple-gray puffballs had moved in closer to me, marching to the south, a dark battalion. It was heavy winds making a whirlpool of the sky. And I braced against its chill.

In all the wild commotion, there came a parting and a path for the lead soprano to take center stage. And she took it, by god. She led with a long high note that set ablaze that dark battalion—turning each little soldier a bright orange-white, as well as the sky from gray to blue, in an epic change of scene. I had to hold my breath throughout the symphonic explosion.

Off to stage left, the tallgrass over by the pond glowed platinum. The dark green leaves of the old oaks glinted like nature-made twinkle lights. So, during the first instrumental break, I straightened my back, as I sat on my Sunrise Stone, and raised both arms in praise of the tuneful glory. I thanked the Great Spirit for the privilege, and for getting me out of bed. For I had been quite comfortable there.

I stayed in that position, dazed, buzzed, and humming, for some time. And then, a phantom appeared in the corner of my eye from the left side. A falcon of some kind, it seemed, with a profoundly white belly and black crown, drifted right up above me, less than ten feet away, and hovered in the heavy breeze there. A breathtaking beauty. A denouement.

I froze, as it drifted over my shoulder. And I asked myself, in careful silence: *What is going on with these birds that keep appearing as benedictions at the end of sacred moments like this?*

First, I remembered the "haunting bird" that "rose, Christ-like, from the stunted piñon trees," when I climbed to the top of Cerro Gordo in Santa Fe.

Next came the "ghost bird" in the Fire Circle on October 1st. In the darkness, I saw it only by firelight. It "swooshed straight over my head from behind…" I wrote, "…so close I heard the air in its wings and tailfeathers." And then, it disappeared into the night.

But again on November 1st, All Saints Day, when I had first discovered the Sunrise Stone, came the red-cockaded woodpecker in the skeleton tree right next to me, as a gentle benediction to my first sunrise service. My opening bout with prayer to the Great Spirit.

And now, this one: the white-bellied phantom that not even my friend Bob Wood, an avid birder for over 50 years, could help identify from the detailed description I gave him. Which has me thinking of how three of the four birds have been mysterious and unidentifiable flying objects that I could only describe as some "cross between" other familiar birds. Maybe a little "shape-shifting" going on in the feathered world?

It does not bother me at all to think of them as spiritual messengers. Nor does it bother me that they delivered no actual messages—outside of their inexplicable timing, unusual appearances, shocking proximity, and numinous presences.

But whatever their purpose may be, I do not see them as accidental. And they are teaching me to keep my eyes open, my soul ever-aware, and my heart available. Like I did the moment the phantom bird disappeared to the north—just as a large bank of clouds moved in and closed the curtain on the morning's opera.

Give Thanks, Dammit

I understand that for some, the holidays are a source of stress, if not depression. They're a call to arms and airports and gas pumps and traffic dead zones. But my family, by the good guidance of my mother, celebrated the season well, and for the right reasons. As I wrote in *The Broken Summer* chapter called "Women's Line:" *Ceremony, food, grace, and gratitude lived at the core of everything.*

So nothing—not a marriage all deflated like some big blow-up Santa Claus lawn ornament laid out flat in a front yard in January, nor my father aching in some mechanical hospital bed in between his physical therapy sessions, nor my beloved country's slide into fascism—is going to keep me from saying thanks over ridiculous portions of mashed potatoes and gravy and green bean casserole this year, dammit.

And nothing's going to stop me from sitting down, alone if I have to, with a bowl of salty popcorn and some spiked eggnog, and watching "A Charlie Brown Thanksgiving" when the big gluttonous feast is over, dammit.

And that's why, here on the day before, I blazed into the grocery store, tossing cans of green beans, pumpkin pie filling, mushroom soup, evaporated milk, water chestnuts, and crispy onions, along with bags of cranberries and brown sugar, an apple, some raisins, eggs, and spices into my cart (but then, backtracked to grab the sliced black olives and pimientos I'd forgotten on Aisle 2), before rolling it all straight up to the self-checkout with well more than 10 ITEMS OR LESS—where I got $40 cash back so I could go buy a decent bottle of tequila—because …
I … am going … to cook, dammit.

And cook I did—all afternoon—with classic Christmas tunes blaring on the stereo. Then afterwards I dressed to the nines, put on the Australian cowboy-ish hat I bought in Santa Fe, and cut a trail to the Continental Club Gallery for the McMurtry show, where I scored a stool in the VIP section at the back bar and sipped on Kellieritas with my small but growing cadre of lady friends, and the odd assortment of other vagabonds and outcasts who come here because their families are not like mine, and so they need to buck up and lubricate before tomorrow's football game and sibling skirmishes—along with my daughter's new boyfriend, no less.

Kellie passed around her still-warm homemade pumpkin muffins to all us regulars, and we broke bread together, then raised our tequilas, whiskeys, and gins in a hopeful toast to our survival, and whatever's on the other side of it.

And we gave thanks, dammit.

Grateful Anyway...

November 24

...grateful that I was able to bring a taste of our family's long traditions—Mom's cornbread dressing, Dad's shoepeg corn salad, the green bean casserole, and my cranberry chutney, along with pumpkin pie that I made from the can's recipe—to Mom and Dad in that dismal rehab room on Thanksgiving morning...

...grateful that—unlike the previous six or seven months—my toes actually get a little chilled when I write by the window in the mornings—to the point I have to consider turning up the heat...

...grateful to be leaving the second season of this long and lonely, life-gouging-yet-liminal year soon...

...grateful for the way the stones don't charge a thing for their friendship—and for the endless hours of fun, meditation, growth, and healing they provide...

…grateful for the one good and sharp
eye that Stoney-the-cat still has—which
appears to be enough for him…

…grateful that both of my sweet parents
continue to recognize me and call me by
my name when I walk into the room…

…grateful for the way Charlie Brown
reminds me we are not the only ones
who get a little saddened, or depressed,
by the holidays now and then…

…grateful for my dear daughter, who is
capering into a new life—a near mythical
creature—my sweet little phoenix, rising
from the ashes of our past…

…grateful for fire and that primal maw
of flames—the thin line that it draws
between light and death, a lifesaving
warmth and severe burn—and how it
reminds me that, with the right set of
basic skills, we could live with, and on,
almost nothing…

…grateful for those who still listen to poetry—but even more so for those who read it when I'm not around to subtly suggest it…

…grateful for my friends who accept my wild passions…the quirk and torque of my thrumming brain…all my literary executions of societal norms, political pricks, and religious prats…the way I take too long to think about how to say something…and even how I prefer the stones, trees, and fire to them…

…and also grateful for everything that I'm forgetting to remember here…

Damn Well

November 26

Dad pushed a button to raise the head of his bed so he could be closer to the rolling tray that had his dinner on it— food as plastic as the plate they put it on. Then, before refusing to eat most of it, he reached for Mom's hand to pull her in nearer to his pallid face. His speech is slurred from the wheelbarrow of drugs they bring him each day. Yet, he managed to get these words out:

I've always been able to adjust to reality.
But I don't know what reality is now.

In combination with the drugs, the daily physical therapy sessions are making him weaker by degrees. I'm noticing a loss of will. He turns 90 next month. He's tired. And he damn well deserves to be—this great, great man that I would say age has brought to his knees, but he doesn't even have the strength to kneel.

That evening, Mom cried as she told me that story and the quote from lunch. I'd brought her back to their assisted living cottage just up I-10 to spend the night with her and pour her a glass of Kendall Jackson chardonnay. Because, she damn well deserves it.

We took our glasses out to the front screened-in porch and bundled up in blankets to sit and watch, and listen to the raucous squawking of, the waddling ducks by the pond across the road.

She went quiet for a time. We took sips among the echoes of that quacked choir. And then, during a lull—brought on by half the flock taking flight—she barely whispered, without turning to look at me: *I don't know where we go from here.*

She turned 91 last June. She's tired too. I hold her hand to steady her when we walk from buildings to cars, and back again. But her incessant worry over him keeps her from taking breaks to get the rest she needs. That's why I bring her to the cottage on the nights when I can. She sleeps there, as long as I'm there sleeping too.

I remember thinking, back in the broken summer: *I'm too old for this stuff. Aren't we supposed to arrive somewhere? And aren't we supposed to figure things out? You know, the Golden Years…and all that crap?*

But my parents, today, have reminded me that *that* is a ridiculous assumption. If not a dangerous idea to believe in.

So, here I am, at 58, trying to adjust to reality. But I don't know what reality is anymore. And I damn well don't know where I go from here.

Fiddler on the Stone

November 28

In the gloaming hour of morning, my daughter came to me in the form of a sunrise. She danced behind a scatter of clouds. And though mostly hidden, she still lit up the sky. Which is best. Stare too long into those eyes, and you'll go blind.

In her normal skin, on normal days, she is 27-and-a-half years old, and she's just moved in with a new beau in a way she's not moved in with one before. This new situation seems, I hesitate to say, normal. And, it makes me nervous in a way I've not been nervous before.

So I stopped fiddling around the Sunrise Stone and sat down on it, instead—so I could think the day in on invisible wings.

Unconsciously, I began to whisper-sing the opening lines to "Sunrise, Sunset," from *Fiddler on the Roof,* where Tevye

stares off into a long flashback scenario
and groan-sings in his *basso profundo*:

> Is this the little girl I carried?
> Is this the little boy at play?
> I don't remember growing older
> When did they?

My shoulders sagged beneath a heavy
sigh. I had to turn and look away from
her. And that's when I saw, in the west,
that my father had come to me as well,
in the form of the Beaver Moon, slowly
setting. He floated silently behind gray-
blue clouds that were busy on their way
to nowhere in particular. He brought to
mind the second verse:

> What words of wisdom can I give
>   them?
> How can I help to ease their way?

I paused to question, through tears, my
new commitment to meet and to spend
more time with sunrises and sunsets. If
things like this keep happening, I'm not
sure how much I'll be able to take.

So I went back to fiddling around the
stone, clearing some weeds and smaller
rocks—my daughter and father looking
over my shoulders. And, well, before too
long, I found myself singing the chorus,
out loud to everyone:

> Sunrise, sunset
> Sunrise, sunset
> Swiftly fly the years
>
> One season following another
> Laden with happiness and tears

Sarah, Larry, & Me

November 30

Traveling state highways on gray-foggy, heavy-misty, light-rainy, low-cloudy days with Sarah McLachlan on the radio sing-wailing:

> *It's comin' on Christmas,*
> *They're cuttin' down trees*

really does set the mellow tone for my Advent Season. I don't know how she can sing so flawlessly while crying. But she sure manages.

I tend to crack up, as my friend Larry would warn you. He makes fun of me, jaded cynic that he is. But I suspect that, secretly, it's his favorite part of my *Fire Pit Sessions*. So we're quite the team. We take turns, saying: *You're the darkness…* the other snapping back: *No,* you're *the darkness.* We should have t-shirts made with arrows pointing at each other: *I'm with the darkness* ➔ / ⬅ *No, I'm…*

The bottom line is that we both, along
with Sarah, wish we had a river we could
skate away on. And we're also in an ongoing competition with her—in that all
three of us believe in the delusion:

> *I'm gonna make a lot of money,*
> *Then I'm gonna quit this crazy scene*

She may be winning that battle. However, when it comes to the lines:

> *But I'm so hard to handle,*
> *I'm selfish and I'm sad*

not one of us is leading, nor lagging. But,
there's one area where they cannot touch
me. I mean, *Don't even bother tryin'*, I huff
to Larry—with my chest all puffed out.
And even though she sings it better than
I do? When it comes to:

> *I made my baby say goodbye...*

man, I'm killin' it.

~ December ~

Back to It

December 1

In the dark-fingered dawn, I park my car just off Gray Street, to get a 2-hour slot. In the 43° and mist, I take the sidewalk to the Gray Owl for coffee, here in my Charlie-Brown-of-a-home-town, and it wells up in me: *I love it. I* love *it. I LOVE this.* This old town of mine covered in a fluttery blanket of fading brown-yellow leaves; the bluster of this almost-winter weather; this funkified coffee shop with huge paper snowflakes and old bicycles hanging from the ceiling; the sad dreams and dregs of all the university's riffraff; the broken hopes of a football season gone bad; the rumble-thundering of a freight train two blocks away; and the gossamer-boned woodnymph behind the counter braiding her black hair into

two waist-length pigtails before dipping
her hands into flour to knead the scone
dough. Yeah…especially her.

But, what I mean more to say is: with a
passion. I love it all deeply…wondrously.
And I love it with a degree and brand of
passion that I have been slowly shaming
out of myself for the last fifteen years—
for reasons hard to explain…but it has
something to do with trying to cram
myself into a different style and way
of being. Nobody's fault but my own.

Now though, the feeling is returning to
my funny bones. (All my bones're funny,
not just one.) I have walked so far in the
wrong direction, I'm coming around the
other side of the planet, to where I am
now finally headed toward the place I
should've gone.

I want it back. I want to love that way
again. And not just my town. Life. Dirt.
Stones. My funny bones. And, everyone
else's, too.

Yes, I want to *hurt* that way again. Like I used to: passionately. Oh sure, I've been lovin' 'n' hurtin' all along. But not with that fun-ol'-fashioned-Nathan-Brown passion…back when I used to frighten people with it…and back when I made people move over to a farther table in a coffee shop like this one, because I was reading a Stephen Dunn or Sharon Olds poem and could not keep to myself my out-loud *Damns!* and *God help me-s!*

I've seen three women in the two hours I've been here, that I *could* have slipped into the bathroom with and eaten alive? With mutual consent, of course. That's who I am. And, nobody has to like it. Including those three women.

And, don't worry, I'm not gonna bother that lovely little wood-nymph behind the counter. But, I am gonna howl down the sidewalk when I leave here, for thinking about how I do still believe: I will find her…somewhere, someday…in a more mature form…down the roads I'm sure to travel.

And why not do it with a passion, and abandon? Can I get an *Amen!* anyone?

And I'm going to roam this wide world just as mad-passionately, too. Because I am a mad-passionate son-of-a-heartland-gun about more than just love and feminine beauty.

I mean, I haven't even gotten around to tequila, yet. So, what I'm getting at here is: *Everything.*

Have I made myself clear?

Plains, Trains, and Memory Lanes

December 2

I went memory shopping yesterday—
just drove around with the car set to
shuffle. I lived in Norman for over 40
years. And I'm staying with friends who
live in the neighborhood where I grew
up—because her parents gave her the
house she grew up in. So I didn't have
to go very far to stir up the past.

I don't linger anymore over the house I
grew up in. It lost its soul to a remodel,
and a tree murder. Arboricide. But, the
house I owned for sixteen years over on
Midway Drive, across the interstate, still
causes me pause. I single-fathered Sierra
in it. And Ashley and I made our start in
its walls. It looks about the same—but
with the trees I planted having sprouted
into gods.

I went on to the nearby pond where we
used to walk Cayenne. This was always
the best time of year for it too. Autumn

is magical here. And Cayenne was the
sweet pup that defined our relationship.
(I now believe our marriage died with
her, late in the first summer of the pandemic.) I slowly began to circle around
the pond and got to thinking about that
old girl. I still miss her. And I'm talking
about the dog, for now.

But, by the time I got to the footbridge
on the far side of her favorite massive
water puddle, always full of ducks, a
thunderstorm had broken out in my
eyes. I was crying like Odysseus at the
end of every chapter. I wanted to go
back. I wanted those days back again,
as useless as that urge ever is. And I'm
not just talking about Cayenne anymore.
I wanted to fix everything—back there
in those years before it was too late.

So now I was dancing with the Devil.
Passionately. Remember what I said in
that last chapter? I also want to *hurt* like
I used to. Full-bodied—without shame
or volcanic suppression. And I know. I
understand the limits of what's possible.

But we bust our brains like this some-times. It can't be helped. And yet I also know what I would not trade to go back, given the opportunity, for the rebirth of my soul that appears to be going on in this up-side-down year.

That's no reason to avoid all of those memories, though—even the ones that twist your intestines into blood-stained knots. So I emotionally limped back to the car and decided to try some other parts of town.

Straight west of Harve Collins Field, where I attended maybe two football games during my high-school-outcast years, runs a small street—Glenwood. And down on the south side, sits the living room floor, behind black bricks, on which I lost my virginity to an older woman. Meaning she was 31, and I was working on a bachelor's degree.

She got fed up one night with me and my religious convictions, and she threw some couch cushions on the floor, then grabbed my front belt-loops and pulled me down on top of her with a shocking strength. Considering she was 5 foot 2.

To my credit, she was also solid muscle. But, how she managed to undress both of us while we were wrestling, remains a mystery. She made it work, though. And then…she made it work.

After my cruise down that memory lane, I drove past First Baptist Church, where Dad had pastored for 30 years, and I felt a brief surge of hell-bound guilt for that long-ago summer night. My God…the sheer number of ways religion raveled my burgeoning brain folds into psychic convolutions.

That church sits half a block from the railroad tracks—the last memory I will bring up. But it breaks my heart that the train's horn blows no more. A new city ordinance. My God again, that long and lonesome moan. That will linger in my mind's ear forever.

If someone ever asks: *So what's the song, the greatest hit, that tops the playlist of your childhood?* That would be it. And now that it sounds no more, I can never, fully, go back home again.

Flames of Hope

December 3

I want to thank the Catholics, and their long tradition of appropriating pagan festivals (in order to relieve the pagans of their overly lascivious amounts of fun and relative nakedness) for turning just the one Eve, and the one Day, of the Christmas I grew up with into a month-long holiday that begins with the Sunday closest to St. Andrews Day—November 30 (the beginning of Advent)—and runs through to the Epiphany, January 6 (the culmination of Christmastide). So, *more* than a month, really.

And I'm craving it more this year than ever. I so need an Advent Season—an arrival, a coming, a time of preparation, anticipation, and waiting. But especially on this First Sunday that is dedicated to Hope. Grant me some of that as well— for I have been greatly lacking in things like hope for some time now.

And, while you're at it, could you grant
some to my mom and dad as well—as
they sit there, in a dank hospital room,
on yet another warm San Antonio day
in December.

But also to my daughter, with respect to
her future world, and the mania of this
country that twists her head all the way
around and back.

And I don't know who I was just talking
to, exactly. But I feel no need to name it
anymore. Nor to label it a her or a him.

No, what I need, here on this beautiful
Sunday, as I raise a fire in praise to this
sun setting into the arms of angels, is
Hope. And I need it somp'n fierce,
dear whoever…or whatever…might
be out there.

That's why I lit a fire, instead of the
proper purple candle, for this holy
opening day. My Advent needs a
bigger flame.

Tie a Knot

December 5

Of course, even in times of hope and yuletide anticipation, there come the days when the pen barely crawls across the page. She flies out to the East Coast on the business of love. So…you find yourself a small rancher for the week, caring for donkeys, cats, and the dog. Sweet beings you care about, and love to care for. Sweet ones who have their own loves for braying and barking, or moaning and meowing, when things aren't done the way mother does it.

And then, your older brother calls, interrupting your morning writing, to discuss for the very first time, the possibility of hospice for Dad. So, with the phone glued to your ear, you go out to distribute the hay and the kibble to all who are in dire need, in order to kill the two proverbial birds with that one hard stone—a silly saying laced with terrible violence.

But also, you do it to distract yourself
from the flood of tears falling from the
dual darknesses in your eyes.

Anyway, by the time you get back to the
journal, the candle, and the coffee-now-
cold, you don't have a damn thing to say
that warrants the sacrifice of trees, nor
the paper they give their lives for. And
you just accept that you can't be "on"
every day.

So you bow, once again, to the hard
truth that you are still just a caterpillar
dissolving in the juices of the cocoon of
transformation. And you recognize, once
again, you must continue to draw from
the deep well of time and patience. Just
hold on. Other days are galloping up
over the horizon in the golden rose
of the sun's dawning.

Tipsy Angels and Fallen Gods

December 6

My daughter and I were 27 years getting
to tonight. The story of our life together
is yet another ode to patience. And she
now reveals to me that the Gift Seed of
"Women's Line" runs in two directions
for me: back to Mom…and forward to
Sierra. I hadn't thought of it before, but
she has become the nurturing female.
She lives head-to-strings, and heart-to-
brush, just like her grandmother. And
she embodies Art as a Sacred Way of
Being—one of the things that makes
us closer than we've ever been.

So tonight we met up at Home Slice on
South Congress in Austin for pieces of
pepperoni pizza that were the size of
baseball pendants sagging over the edge
of paper plates. We were dressed against
the chill it takes Texas till December to
reach. And we reveled in the warm
cheese and burnt crust of it all.

Conversation is automatic for us now. And for all the time we did not get to spend together in her earlier years, our similarities shock me. Subatomics must be involved. She's an artist, to her core. She feels, loves, and hurts with the same passion. And she is a dreamer…to the point of sometimes dangerous.

After pizza, we walked down Congress to the fire escape stairs that lead up to some of the best music in town. Kellie let us in upon the magic knock. We took my bay window seat by the bar—but not before some selfies on the famous stage with the "Continental" sign behind us and McMurtry's guitars at our knees.

She and Kellie had not seen each other since before Sierra was legal to drink. So it was a proud moment for us all. And, just before the doors opened, Kellie ceremoniously made her an amaretto sour with an orange slice on the rim.

Then, as Kellie slid me my Kellierita, Sierra beat me to the punch putting a credit card down to start the tab. She beamed at the two of us and said, *I like my new job.* Kellie raised her eyebrows and took the card to the register.

My daughter is beautiful—which puts me in the unfortunate demographic of looking like a dirty old man when we hit the town together. It's been a problem for years. So, I made a deliberate point to introduce her to all the regulars. You know…to help dispel any increasingly inebriated notions and misgivings. She was instantly popular. A gift she has.

During the show, we sat, sipped, and ribbed each other in reaction to James's extraordinary, to-the-point-of-pissing-off-other-writers, lyrics. Now and then, she would sing the harmonies with that angelic voice of hers. Kellie patched us up midway through. And then, toward the end, Sierra drifted off on her own to the back bar and effortlessly slid into the small sea of VIPs. No need for me now. Another gift she has.

As I gazed over at the dark-red neon
scene across from me, a quiet thought
came to me: We did it. She did it. I did
it. For all my failings, and all her stormy
experiments in breaking free, over there
stood a glorious and monumental *getting-
it-rightness.*

So I tipped my hat to some invisible god
I felt sure was near me, and whispered:

Yeah…thanks for that one.

Sit with It

December 7

Slowly, over the jagged arc of my life, but particularly in the last two decades, I came to know myself by way of what I perceived to be *wrong* with me—those parts of me that didn't fit with society, or the other people I was forced to live, learn, and work around. It became a bad habit, as well as the source of my humor.

I soaked up what the mean kids on the playground said about sissiness. I took on the guilt of what the church told me about my hopeless attractions to the glories of the female human form. I believed what the pundits and dour prognosticators preached about the Dow Jones, retirement plans, credit scores, work hours, and benefits. And in marriage? Well, I won't go into that. But anyone who's been, or happens to be, married, probably has some idea of what I would say.

And so, after a lifetime of encrypted programming and unconscious absorption, it is no laughing matter to one day find yourself standing at the cliff edge of the key question: *What if they're all wrong?*

A question that has a little nuclear family of questions that it lives with: What if it's okay to be a renter, instead of an owner? What if more and bigger are not better? What if capitalism isn't the best system? What if erotic yearning is beautiful biology, instead of grounds for an eternity in Hell? And hey, what if having certain feminine qualities only makes me more wholly masculine?

The more I sit with myself—which is happening a lot lately—the more I like me exactly the way I am. No…I mean *love* who I am. And the longer I bathe in this revelation, the easier it gets to raise my head, point my forefinger, and say, to whoever's left in the room with me:

And you can take it…or leave it.

Natural Selection

December 8

I have tried a hundred ways to describe and explain the extraordinary impact of my youngest days as a Highly Sensitive Child. One new way to say it might be: I had a happy, normal, Southern Plains childhood that permanently scarred my psyche.

I took on way too much, way too early. Seemingly small occurrences could feel to me like they would have lifelong consequences. And I've too often said that in my kindergarten through 12th-grade education, I roamed the tiled halls and sat behind those tiny desks (that were made for righthanders) in dull fluorescent classrooms, muttering to myself:

Who are these people? And why am I here?

So, it thrilled me to come across the written version of the bully scenario in *A Christmas Story* that is more detailed in

Jean Shepherd's short story "Grover Dill and the Tasmanian Devil." Get a load of this opening sentence:

> The male human animal, skulking through the impenetrable fetid jungle of Kidhood, learns early in the game just what sort of animal he is.

He closes that paragraph with this:

> He daily does battle with horrors and emotions that he will spend the rest of his life trying to forget or suppress. Or recapture.

Oh man. Someone who gets it! I still feel those hot emotions when certain types of men walk into the bar—guys whose dirty psyches developed a skip in the LP of their lives somewhere around the fifth grade, and no one ever came along to lift the needle out of their warped groove.

And, of course, it doesn't help that the "impenetrable fetid jungle" we continue

to try to survive in, never gets any less
impenetrable—nor fetid. We just get a
little better at spotting who to avoid at
all costs.

But still, in spite of my age and best
efforts, here I stand, once again, on the
rowdy playground of my old nightmares,
just waiting for the other untied sneaker
to drop.

Breaking the Fourth Wall

It's been happening around the tables of old friends. It happened last night by the flicker of flames in the Fire Circle with my daughter. It's even happened out on the front porch of the cottage with Mom over glasses of wine. Hell, it's happening around the tables and fireplaces of fairly new friends.

It's a strange little odyssey of increasing honesty breaking through the previous hesitancies of these others who've been observing me from an objective distance and a broader perspective that I never could've achieved, by virtue of being mostly in my body.

They begin by raising their eyebrows and starting their sentences with things like:

You know, Nathan... or, *Well, we always wondered...* or, *We never could quite understand...*

It's become such a pattern, I now brace myself for it whenever a second glass of anything is poured.

Turns out, there've been a lot of shaking heads and scratched hairlines behind my back for some time. Maybe loving…but shaking and scratching nonetheless.

Best I can piece together, I have been acting in an avant-garde play with a plot no one could figure out. And for some of them, it's even been long-running in the theatre of the absurd.

A few friends with academic tendencies have panned the performance. But, that is what they do. It's required by the ivory tower system. And I stopped taking that personally decades ago.

The stark details and summaries aren't necessary. And while I haven't taken the Hippocratic Oath, officially, it's feeling more and more important to me now to "First, do no harm." Whatever the other actors in this psycho-drama may, or may not, have been responsible for, the only thing that really matters from here on is that I acknowledge, and deal with, the part I have played.

Things got far too Shakespearean, I'm afraid. Love was doomed. Trap doors opened. People got hurt.

There was no poison involved. No throats were slit. But it all came down, nonetheless—just before the curtain crashed to the stage.

Was it a tragedy? Or a comedy? The best are usually both. But either way, I've got my agent looking for a new story.

A New Role

December 10

It was a classic story, my life before this one. Divorced ten years. The first three of which, I did not date—because the psychologist said it would be better for my daughter. Then came the very first attempt at dating, which, within weeks, descended into some Hollywoodesque psychothriller starring Michael Douglas and Glenn Close. Yes, *Fatal Attraction* was a movie from the 1980s I should have paid attention to.

After the dust and fear settled from that one, I had a few more relationships that were mere disasters. Then along came a young, sweet, thoughtful woman who messed with my cynicism. We dated for four years. So it's not like we rushed into where angels fear for us to tread. Which was asking her to marry me. Something she was not pushing for. Oh…I believe she loved me. But there was a sign there I should've read more closely.

Anyway, we worked at it. We watched Hallmark movies at Christmastime— great examples of how *new* love works. But, eventually, cracks formed in our plot. I kept believing, like the movies. And she tried, for a long time.

It's a story. Not uncommon. But a fairy-tale for which she wants to rewrite the ending. And all I can do is contemplate my edited role and determine, very carefully, how I want to play the smaller part she's offering. Will I be a villain? Or will I be gracious? Goodhearted? Or Stoic? Will I fall into this autumn? Will I rise somewhere beyond it? Or maybe even above it, come spring?

Well, whatever characteristics I choose, I've got to act my way through the approaching winter. And so, I'll need to constantly remind myself: there are an unlimited number of other stories to live, write, and tell.

Kiva Time

With the approach of solstice and the Cold Moon, I've hit the road for Santa Fe. I need some kiva time, for winter dreaming.

I turned in grades yesterday and am done with online teaching until late January. And I'm wrapping up three book projects for other people on my press, while letting everyone know I won't be accepting any more.

I am pulling in. I'm tuning out. At least where the news and noise of the market-driven madness of the great American machine is concerned. I'm going to go deeper into the cocoon.

I need to rest. And I want to waste good time reading, and wandering. I'm going to let the flâneur in me have his way. I will travel slow, and let the Earth rise to meet me.

I'm also going to listen more, and better, to the mostly unheard around me—and lend my ear solely to the voices of those I trust.

Yes, the next few moons will be a quiet overture for the springtime of a fresh storyline in my odyssey.

So, I invite you to lean in closer to the fire with me during these days and wrap a blanket around your shoulders. Maybe bring along a favorite book of poetry… and grab a glass of wine to go with it, if you're so inclined. (But I'll have tequila, of course.) Whatever works for you.

But let's cross over into the next season together.

A Letter to My Daughter

December 12

My Sierra,

I need to put this in ink on the page for you. To give it a wax seal. It's much too important just to talk about at dinner, or over drinks on your back porch.

I failed you too many times over the last two decades. I put other obligations and someones above you in critical moments and situations. And, I allowed my loves for those other someones to cloud over my truer responsibility to LOVE itself— the Big-Whole-LOVE that should super- sede all else.

To put it plainly, I should have stood up for you. I should have stood up for us. And I should have stood up for me, for that matter. I should have said No when it was called for. I should have drawn lines and said: *This far…no further.*

So, this letter is my solemn word to you:
I am putting you first again. The way it
was, and is, meant to be. And I will not
let any other love (with the small-case
"l") ever interfere with us again.

I may falter, here and there, now and
then. But from this time forward, you
have full and final authority to call me
on it if I do.

I love you…

Dad

100,000 Possibilities

December 13

I have never met anyone altogether un-interesting at Paul's house. He lives in Aldea, a small satellite community out northwest of Santa Fe. At least for now. Paul moves around a lot. He plays real estate roulette very well. But I'm always meeting people at Paul's various houses. And they tend to range from quite fun, to interesting, to super cool—or some combination.

Last night, he introduced me to Scott and Alan. They quickly seemed to be fellow "travelers" of mind, spirit, and the road. And Scott happened to bring with him a little phrase game called Pep Talk Builder. It consists of four columns with each one containing eighteen brief phrases that have a small blue checkbox before each one. Column one lists fun openers. Columns two and three offer effervescent encouragements. And then column four is meant to supply the mic-drop of an ending, where you point the Cousin Eddie finger and say: *Bingo.*

Scott checked a zigzag of four boxes on one for me that reads: ☒ The word is out: ☒ your radiant personality ☒ is the stuff of dreams, ☒ it's just a fact. (Scott knows nothing about me. But still, I felt grateful for his first impression.)

The ones he checked for Paul—whom he knows a bit better—said, ☒ Bestie, ☒ the way you think ☒ turns to gold, ☒ capiche? And then Alan's added up to: ☒ Hey pal, ☒ that pizazz you have ☒ stops traffic, ☒ everybody says so.

By this point, I wanted to explain why one should never put games like this in front of a poet—at least not if you want him to pay close attention to the rest of the evening's conversations—because now, he is staring at a clean page and checking boxes in his mind. Because a poet wants to be in charge of phrasing for himself, thank you very much.

So I started piecing together my own zigzag of pep talks:

☒ Rumor has it… ☒ your overall aesthetic ☒ makes the sun jealous, ☒ at least that's what I heard.

Or: ☒ Hear ye, hear ye: ☒ your modus operandi ☒ makes angels sing, ☒ can you deal with that?

I soon forced myself to pull back and walk away. There was nowhere for this game to go but south. I mean, the small print at the top of the page claims "Over 100,000 combinations possible." And so, my English major brain doesn't have the capacity for that kind of math.

That's why I settled myself down and grabbed my margarita to go rejoin the conversation over on the couch. Which was fun and interesting, and occasionally even super cool.

Home for Christmas

December 14

Sitting at a small table in the bar at Maria's—because the five stools at the bar itself are stuffed with a loud herd of greasy dudes who are not appreciating it the way I would—I'm calculating up that I've made seven trips to or through New Mexico this year. That might be a record for me. And December is definitely the month to end the streak on.

There's snow on the ground and in the trees. The streets are a muddy-mushy mess. Temperatures are in the 30s and 40s. Farolitos line the upper rims of the adobe walls, all lit up. And tourists kick back into a more low-key wintry mode and don't parade their otherness as much.

The smell of burning piñon fills the air with its one-of-a-kind grace. And a low-riding sun throws a cool light that would make Georgia O'Keeffe twist and turn

in her grave. And all over this town,
even the enchiladas and chile rellenos
come "Christmas," if you know how to
order them.

There are other beautiful places around
the world. But not one exactly like this.
God lingered for a while over northern
New Mexico when he was creating the
Earth. He knew he had a good thing
going here. He knew he was on fire.

Anyway, Sinatra is crooning "I'll Be
Home for Christmas" on the ceiling
speakers. And I'm musing over the new
truth that wherever I am, I will be home
for Christmas. Because, wherever I am,
The Sky will be above me. Just knowing
that, gives me some peace.

And this DK La Ultima margarita, with
a salty rim, doesn't hurt the cause either.

Sailing into Winter

December 15

As the long-dark at the end of autumn
applies the brakes, soon to yield to the
sun's revving engine, I pack my psychic
bags for the winter leg of this year's hard
journey. And space is limited. So, I allow
only the absolute necessities.

For starters, I bought two dozen Sakura
Micron pens with sepia ink—the fuel.
And, to go with them, a stack of blank
journals—no lines allowed. I said blank.
They're the tanks waiting to be filled.

Then, I check the air pressure, tread, and
authenticity of each book in the carefully
selected library of poetry and prose that
will carry me. They're the tires the whole
thing rolls on. So, if you don't take good
care of them, the writing goes flat.

I've cleaned the windshields of three
pairs of reading glasses and have them
stored and ready to go.

I polished the beautiful burnished-brass compass Ashley gave me. Because, even if you don't know where you are going, it's good to have a sense of the direction you're taking.

The Gift Seeds sit, all tied-up and snug inside the doe-skin pouch Christopher sent them in, providing their ongoing promise of transformational guidance and grounding.

I have some candles to keep the light of the spirit glowing around me—as well as plenty of matches to light them, and the fires that will keep me warm in the cold months ahead.

My good hiking boots will get me back out into the wild embraces of the Earth, bringing me back to the sources of all things, along with the life-reviving teachings of the other-than-human world. It's time to attend a better school.

I'm throwing in sunscreen and broad-brimmed hats, as well as my expensive

polarized sunglasses, because the hard
truths of the sun's philosophy burn.

And I'll need nuts, seeds, raisins, and
snack bars to keep the brain running—
and because cafés and restaurants break
the budget and beltline.

Oh, and maybe some dark chocolate for
the soul. On those longer, more desolate
stretches of road, you need at least one
delicious thing you can still believe in.

The main rule here? No ballast. I am
sailing light under the empyrean ocean
of my new home, The Sky.

It's Official

December 16

It happened, last evening, under the Christmas lights in the plaza, as I was sitting on a cold metal bench next to four young indigenous men prayer-chanting to the steady heartbeat of a handheld skin drum—the song much older than this town that has been here for over 400 years—a song that should not be lost to time and the atrocities of digital music platforms.

I was thinking back over the day—the sunrise I sat very still with as it broke on the dark shoulder of Cerro Gordo Peak, slicing through the chill and piñon trees. Then the afternoon, when I met my soul friend, Riha, another one of my mentor-healers, who drove up from Placitas to sit with me at the bar in Maria's for two hours...where we fixed the world...and where a young apprentice bartender was baffled that I knew the small tattoo on his neck was an outline of Sonora, the

194

Mexican state of his birth…and where the veteran head waiter put a hand on each of our stools to talk to us for ten minutes, because we had admired his blazingly red and white dinner jacket. He had lost 120 pounds and was very proud to be able to fit into it again this Christmas, after years of hard work.

Later on, I'd gone for a long walk down Paseo de Peralta in the early evening and noticed a sign in front of the Travel Bug Bookstore for a storytelling event. So I slipped into the back and up behind the surprisingly large crowd, where I caught out the corner of my eye my longtime compadre in the arts, Navé, who was hosting and filming the show.

When he noticed me, he left his post to come over and hug me. Which is when Regina spotted me and waved hi in the middle of telling her story to the now quizzical crowd. I had given her a ride to a party at Paul's house one night— actually, one of my house concerts— because her night vision was starting

to fail. She'd loved my show and so was
pleased I was getting to see her in action.

When Navé went up at the end to thank
everyone for coming, he apologized for
the scene he'd caused, but explained it
was because "the awesome poet and
singer-songwriter Nathan Brown" had
made an unexpected appearance earlier.
Everyone turned. And I half-waved, all
flushed in the face.

After I thanked him for the kind words
with a quick nod over the milling heads,
I stepped out the back and meandered
toward the plaza. As I came up behind
St. Francis Cathedral, the 6:00 p.m. bells
rang out to call the faithful to recite the
Angelus—bells that ring in my memory
as far back as it goes…bells that have
known me longer than most people in
my life.

So, when I passed La Fonda on the
corner of Old Santa Fe Trail and San
Francisco, where Mom and Dad loved a
certain table and the cheese enchiladas at

La Plazuela—the restaurant where I asked Ashley to marry me—I felt an urge to find a spot to sit down for a while. My soul and bones felt heavy.

And that's when I found the bench near the center of the plaza, and took it. The steady pulse of the skin drum and their ancient monotone, wailing there beneath the multi-colored canopy of lights, were the perfect scene and setting for the profound revelation that was forming in the bubbling cauldron of my mind…

I belong here.

After more than 50 years of loyalty, love, devotion, reverence, learning the culture, and deep listening to the beating heart of this town, and the blood in the stones of the surrounding land, I deserve honorary citizenship here. For decades I've been sensitive to the belief that I am only a guest in New Mexico. But no more.

So right there, on that bench, Santa Fe and I exchanged our vows. No need for

any paperwork. I'm not worried about
the documentation. And there was no
reception afterwards. All our friends
will find out soon enough.

And since this place offers some of the
best Sky in the world, I now claim it to
be a part of what I call and consider:

Home.

Magic Glasses

December 17

I've seen several impossible faces here in Iconik Coffee this morning. Every other time I lift my latte, another one walks in. I'm steering clear of words like *beautiful*, because that's not what I'm talking about. And yet…it is.

But something in my vision has shifted. A rapidly-growing, and a wildly-various, number of eyes, cheekbones, lips, necks, shoulders, hips, and legs utterly enthrall me now—as if in some mysterious fog-enshrouded cave, I discovered a pair of magical glasses in a glowing crystal box, and the moment I tried them on, they disappeared and became a part of me.

I suddenly see every individual human being as wondrously unique and madly distinctive in the arrangement of their features. A thing maybe we all know, instinctively, on some level. But this is different. It's like a Hall of Mirrors at a carnival, except that each mirror makes everyone reflected much more exquisite. (And I'm drinking coffee right now, not tequila.)

For instance, I just saw a young girl who looked *exactly* like Mulan. Only ten times as—I'll go ahead and use it—*beautiful* as any exaggerated and animated stereotype that Disney could dream up. She looked, simply…impossible.

Traveling through the world and walking its streets as a Flâneur, will never be the same. Because I cannot take the glasses off. Because I cannot see or feel them.

I am not complaining…I'm just over-whelmed as I adjust to this new way of seeing. And I'm guessing it's some side-effect of the rearranging and reforming of my metamorphic goo in the chrysalis of my old caterpillar self. But, whatever it is, I'm holding on for dear life, friends, to these crazy reins.

Soft Bullets

The reason for this trip out to the high desert took me down to the Presbyterian Church in Placitas, a small village north of Albuquerque that sits in the morning shadows of the Sandia Mountains. You don't pass through Placitas. No, you go there for some purpose. And mine, this time, was the 26th Annual Winter Solstice Poetry Event.

My current small town, Wimberley, is a "Dark Sky Community." People are encouraged to eliminate, or turn off, or at least shade and point down, all outdoor lighting at night. It has to do with migrating birds and basic human decency. Placitas, though, appears to me to be a "Total Darkness Community."

With my car headlights, I sort of figured out where to park in the gravel lot of the church. From there, however, I had no idea where an entrance to the building might be. Fortunately, someone showed up with his flashlight and pointed it at a set of stairs. He told me the door would be at the top of those.

Once inside, the foyer was large, well-lit, warm, and full of art on the walls. Many of the people milling about seemed not quite sure where to stand or what to do with themselves—which is one way to spot a gathering of poets, bless our shy hearts. But the kind woman in charge of the event knew what to expect and took good care in herding the lot of us over into the main auditorium.

That room was relatively unadorned, in an ascetic, yet cozy way. The pews were hard and unforgiving wood that brought back too many butt-numbing memories for me. The lights were dimmed, which amplified the lovely glow of the electric candles placed in every arched window niche, creating a peaceful, unpretentious air that put my recovering Baptist bones at ease.

When the reading began, they brought
the lights as far down as they possibly
could, without extinguishing them, in
keeping with the Placitas code. Then,
Reverend Tom Ulrich stepped up to a
black music stand with a small clip-on
lamp that wouldn't quite be enough for
anyone to read by. He cheated, though,
by using a backlit iPad for his introduc-
tion. But still, his intro was spot on, and
he ended with fabulous excerpts from a
Victor Hernández Cruz poem—with
stanzas that bled in the air, like:

> when poems start to
> knock down walls to
> choke politicians
> when poems scream &
> begin to break the air

or the last four lines:

> a true poet aiming
> poems & watching things
> fall to the ground
>
> it is a great day

I mean…what were we supposed to do
after that?

He then lit a big candle, that was real, on
a pedestal by the podium, returned to his
seat and, one by one, the poets got up to
read in the prescribed order. Jacque, the
kind organizer, had asked us to pause 20
seconds between readers—and to please
just give our name, the poem's title, and
then read it. Which several of the poets
ignored, because poets have always believed they are the exception to every
rule.

And yet, the evening flowed smoothly.
And after I had read, early in the lineup,
I settled down and into the dark end of
my hard pew, and a beautiful calm came
over me. My mind's camera panned out,
and I saw and sensed the bigger picture
of what was going on.

The scene was reverent. There was an
utmost quietness to it. And the poets,
despite a few needless introductions,
were spot on to the occasion. Their

poems were soft bullets of truth and
art—each one hitting its poetic mark.
And the setting itself felt preindustrial.
It had something of the Old Southwest
to it.

And, once again, I was struck with an
honest sense of awe…for the hopeless
determination and unwavering belief of
poets in their mission. Here, in a packed
room of a small village church, we raised
the Flag of Humanity. Tonight was a leg
for the Earth to stand on. And so, I left
there with my feet firmly on the ground
of who I am…and what I do.

Mandala Morning

December 19

On the last morning in Santa Fe, I took my usual seat up in the front row of the sunrise show. It's by a perfectly-placed picture window next to the fireplace in the living room. A spot that is hard to leave, if you bring a hot cup of coffee with you.

A bright crown of clouds told me that the curtain was about to rise. And so I nestled in, tucked my feet up, and gazed at the purple blood of the shadowed side of the mountains.

When the blazing solar tip cleared the line, just to the north of Cerro Gordo, I had to turn my face a bit to the left to avoid the retina-burn. And that is when I saw, reflected in the window, the two dark-brown seeds of my eyes. They were floating, bodyless little laser beams cutting through a blurry gray fog.

Then, as more of the sun began to peer
over the ridge, the soft yellow-orange of
skin slowly began to fill in around the
edges of the eyes, as if being painted
on by some invisible brush.

By half-rise, the eyebrows and the thin
outline of lips appeared—as if the gray
fog were clearing. I could feel the blood
warming in my cheeks. A soft life-energy
radiated in the bones behind them. I was
a human mandala, emerging. And soon,
there I was: a clear, full-faced reflection
in that pane of glass.

And sometimes, a metaphor will come
along, so plain, so obvious, it's almost
embarrassing. But I didn't make it up;

it was done to me. I had just wanted to watch the sun rise over the spine of the Sangre de Cristos on my final morning here. Does it happen to be a coincidence that I believe a new sun is now rising on my life. And that my true self…my Soul Being…is slowly beginning to appear?

What I know is that a rushing surge of peacefulness came over me—like a dam had broken upriver of my mind. It roiled all around me. It washed all through me, as if some force were breathing life into that mandala. Both eyes were now well-springs of tears. My body shook in the power of it. And how I kept from spilling my coffee, I can't quite say.

The moment did not cure me of my heartache. It didn't usher me into the kingdom of Everything Is Fine Now. The Journey is far from over. But I'm collecting up these sundry miracles, like little cosmic eggs, and placing each one down inside my soul-basket—this new, ever-expanding mandala of my rebirth. And someday, I'll have enough for a feast.

A Benediction

It took Carl Jung 32 years to build his
"Tower" in Bollingen, Switzerland.
He said of the work that it was:

> a kind of representation in stone
> of my innermost thoughts and of
> the knowledge I had acquired…
> a confession of faith in stone.

He considered it a sanctuary, a retreat
for contemplation, a physical means to
deal with his brain-on-fire days of wild
dreams, visions, ghosts, and developing
his ideas and theories, or his "stream of
fantasies," that eventually became the
Red Book. He went on to say:

> From the beginning I felt the
> Tower as in some way a place of
> maturation…in which I could
> become what I was, what I am
> and will be. It gave me a feeling as
> if I were being reborn in stone.

So it is that I spent the entire last day of the Fallen Autumn outside among, and working on, my own stone walls and towers—continuing to be reborn. My sanctuary. An altar that ever upward reaches for my Home. A monument beneath and to The Sky. My very own "confession of faith in stone." Yes, a Bollingen, where, as Jung put it:

> I am in the midst of my true life,
> I am most deeply myself.

I am doubly fortunate in that I feel the exact same way about the act and art of writing—the alphabet being an eternal field full of literary stones.

So…you take a day, like today, where I spend the early morning with coffee and crayons, pens and blank pages, eggs and Tommy Potts' homemade sausage gravy, with all of the big windows thrown wide open…then follow that with stones and bones, cedar and saws, work boots and bottles…followed by sipping a margarita by the flames of a ceremonial fire in the pit of my making...and, well, you can just wrap me up and put a bow on my head. Or you could just roast me alive and call it a good life.

Whatever you choose, I raised my glass up over the flames to toast the waxing Cold Moon—the Long Night Moon.

For so long, I've quietly dreaded this night for being the end to my favorite season of every year. But on this spin around the sun, the deep honest-to-godness is...

I'm ready for this particular Autumn to be behind me. Maybe next year I can be sad in the old way, for the old reason... which I would prefer to this new way, for the new reason...that makes me even more sad.

For now, though, I have the blessings of 10,000 stones, glowing in the dark from a benediction of moon and fire. They will carry me to and through the third season...the Hidden Winter ahead.

And so, come the inevitable morning of tomorrow's solstice, I shall tip my hat to Old Man Winter, and to ancient Boreas, that ol' purple-winged Greek god of the north wind, with his icy breath. (May they both have mercy on me.)

And may I face that frigid breeze with dignity and determination…then brace myself for whatever it blows and brings in with it, along the vagabond way.

May I continue to reach toward a truer life on the other side of all that is behind me. And may you and I both find it deep within ourselves to keep our heads held up, our shoulders pulled back, and our eyes peeled down the road for signs of hope, health, and maybe even a portion of happiness.

Be quiet now: entrust the future
to the gods.

~ *The Odyssey*
Book 19:502-3

Also by Nathan Brown

The Broken Summer
The Pandemic Poems Project
Just Another Honeymoon in France
100 Years
An Honest Day's Prayer
An Honest Day's Ode
An Honest Day's Confession
I Shouldn't Say…
Arse Poetica
Apocalypse Soon
Don't Try (with Jon Dee Graham)
My Salvaged Heart
To Sing Hallucinated
Oklahoma Poems, and Their Poets
Less Is More, More or Less
Karma Crisis: New and Selected Poems
Letters to the One-Armed Poet
My Sideways Heart
Two Tables Over
Not Exactly Job
Ashes over the Southwest
Suffer the Little Voices
Hobson's Choice

Author Bio

Nathan Brown is an author, songwriter, and award-winning poet who lives nowhere in particular, for now. He holds a PhD in English and Journalism from the University of Oklahoma and taught there for over 20 years. He also served as Poet Laureate for the State of Oklahoma in 2013 and 2014.

He's published over 25 books. Among them is *Don't Try*, a collection of poems co-written with songwriter and Austin Music Hall-of-Famer, Jon Dee Graham. His *Oklahoma Poems, and Their Poets* anthology was a finalist for the Oklahoma Book Award. *Karma Crisis: New and Selected Poems* was a finalist for the Paterson Poetry Prize and the Oklahoma Book Award. His earlier book, *Two Tables Over*, won the 2009 Oklahoma Book Award. He has also released several CDs of original music.

For more, go to: brownlines.com

MEZCALITA
PRESS

An independent publishing company
dedicated to bringing the printed poetry,
fiction, and non-fiction of musicians
who want to add to the power and reach
of their important cultural voices.

Visit us at: www.mezpress.com

www.ingramcontent.com/pod-product-compliance
Lightning Source LLC
Chambersburg PA
CBHW031019160726
47991CB00005B/1782